THE BUSINESS
OF BOOK PUBLISHING

THE BUSINESS

OF

BOOK PUBLISHING

BY

CLIVE BINGLEY

PERGAMON PRESS

Oxford · New York · Toronto
Sydney · Braunschweig

Pergamon Press Ltd., Headington Hill Hall, Oxford

Pergamon Press Inc., Maxwell House, Fairview Park, Elmsford,
New York 10523

Pergamon of Canada Ltd., 207 Queen's Quay West, Toronto 1

Pergamon Press (Aust.) Pty. Ltd., 19a Boundary Street,
Rushcutters Bay, N.S.W. 2011, Australia

Vieweg & Sohn GmbH, Burgplatz 1, Braunschweig

First edition 1972

Library of Congress Catalog Card No. 71–187175

Printed in Great Britain by A. Wheaton & Co., Exeter

08 016844 2

CONTENTS

LIST OF ILLUSTRATIONS

ACKNOWLEDGEMENTS

The author would like to thank George Depotex for his encourage-
ment to write this book and his comments on the manuscript,
Hugh Burrell for necessary corrections to Chapter 3, and Carole
Lusty for typing most of the draft and finished manuscripts, no less
than those many friends and acquaintances in the book world who
have contributed willy-nilly to the opinions and experience upon
which this book is founded. The index was compiled by Carolyn
Shercliff.

INTRODUCTION

IN INDUSTRY in general, mid-twentieth-century technological advance
has had, as one of its consequences, the effect of coalescing a multiplicity of small industrial units into large and often broadly based
cartels. It is not my purpose to discuss the economic and political
causes of this, but simply to take the fact as a starting-point.

Book publishing is an industry which has been, traditionally, slow
to adopt new business methods and techniques, but it is now perforce
moving towards a similar consolidation of small independent imprints
into groups of a size more readily able to withstand economic policies
and attitudes which governments are increasingly gearing to a large-
business situation—the control and availability of capital, the emphasis on sophisticated and expensive systems of production and distribution, the deliberate wastage of financial resources on non-financial
(often social) objectives, the shifts in taxation policy, and the incur-
sions into the industrial sphere by governmental action and dictate.

Book publishing, however, has always been a 'personal' business—
one in which the practitioners have invariably possessed some degree
of personal involvement with their products, and with the nature of
their products—books—such as is hardly possible if you make, say,
nuts and bolts, or forged steel valves. This is at the same time one of
the strengths and the weaknesses of the industry; a strength because
in publishing 'quality control' is a subjective matter, dependent upon
the aesthetic or intellectual judgement of the publisher, and not upon
machines capable of measuring the constituents of a piece of metal; a
weakness because the intellectual judgement so often, in the tempera-
ment of man, takes precedence over the commercial, and publishing
is, in the first and last resort, a commercial activity—you make a
profit or you go bust!

It is perhaps because of this intellectual involvement with the product, not just with the management of the operation, that the development of large publishing companies with fixed and separated departments, with advanced systems controlling much of the routine operation, has thrown up more than most other industries a number of people who find the structured life of a big group too frustrating and too far removed from any engagement with its product, and who seek as a consequence either to return to the personal level of publishing by starting on their own, or to remain there by resisting the persuasive arguments for takeover by a group.

There are other reasons too, of course, not least the comparative paucity of top jobs in any publishing firm. But publishing is a business in which a small independent can thrive, both because the basic proportions of the activity remain the same whatever its scale of operation (a large firm is, in one sense, only an amalgam of several small firms), and because the actual physical manufacture of a book is subcontracted to a printer and a bookbinder, so that although capital is needed to pay for the manufacture, it immediately secures a saleable product, without further advance investment in expensive plant or machinery.

One other reason why it is possible to start and maintain a small firm is, paradoxically, the decline in importance of the book in the communications industry as a whole. This will be discussed in some detail in Chapter 1, for it is the purpose of this book to show first the industry's situation in the 1970s and then how the opportunity for small imprints, which are independent to some degree at least, is widening, and thus to define the role which the individual publisher can fill as an adjunct of the larger processes of communication. It is intended in part as an analysis of the book industry, and as an introductory manual to the techniques of small-scale book publishing based on the conclusions of that analysis.

I do not solicit a readership only of would-be independent publishers. If my premise of the decline of books in the communication process is correct, book publishing will have to cater increasingly for sectional markets, and the 'small publisher' concept will be as relevant in large publishing groups as in one-man businesses, and will influence all the associates of the book world—authors, printers, booksellers, and librarians. It may also be that the main theme—the role of the 'small man'—will have some application to other fields of industry.

At the present time there exists the general conviction among British publishers that, on the whole, things have never been better for the book industry. Turnover keeps going up, education and leisure are booming, profits are at last beginning to reach levels comparable with those in other industries. I do not wish in this book to cast a Cassandra-like gloom over the optimism. But implicit in the following text is the belief that communications in society are close to a quite dramatic and technologically based turning-point, and that if the publishing industry refuses in its present contentment to scent these winds of change, it may miss the real opportunity to participate in the future of communications. It depends, first of all, on whether you regard 'the book' as a cultural entity in its own right, or as a form of packaging for communicated thought. If the former, read no further.

CHAPTER 1

THE BOOK INDUSTRY

THE urge to communicate is a fundamental facet of the human condition. The book industry is a commercial consequence of that urge. Whether it is always a wise urge is another matter, and the same reservation applies to some of the activities of the book industry.

The book in its present form as a physical entity dates from less than 1000 years ago. In anything like its present form as a commercial entity it dates effectively from the invention of mechanical printing in the fifteenth century. In many civilisations before that 'publishers' existed as the employers of hired or slave copyists who transcribed in multiples from the dictation of a text, and they sold the resulting scrolls throughout whatever at the time constituted the civilised world. But their economics scarcely relate in any realistic way to the modern book industry, and it is with the development of the mass-produced book that we are concerned—the first product to suffer mechanical mass-production for commercial purposes.

Publishing started as printing—as manufacture rather than dissemination. It was not until the nineteenth century that publishers really began to exist in their own right as promoters (in the broad sense) of the printed word, instead of being printer/booksellers ('stationers') selling only or mainly their own productions. Before that the printing, publishing and bookselling functions were all exercised together by the same individual or group of individuals. (The word 'publish' simply means 'to make available to others'—a definition which summarises the essence of the publisher's job without revealing any of its practical implications.) And in those days, when no organised form of

1

national or even local network of distributive outlets existed, it was naturally prudent that the usual course for a producer of a book or pamphlet should be to 'subscribe' the venture to buyers of copies (who 'subscribed' their names on a list) before embarking upon the printing, so that the true number of copies needed was known before the risk was taken.

'Subscription' remains in the trade today as the term used for blandishments exercised by publishers upon booksellers (not readers) to commit themselves before publication of a book to the purchase of a certain number of copies. But it mostly takes place after the book has been printed, and so seldom has much effect on the number of copies issued in the edition. Its main influence, indeed, tends to be on the financial security of the booksellers thus blandished!

It was natural that the proliferation of commerce in the late eighteenth and early nineteenth centuries, in no small measure due to the growth of transport, should change the emphasis of the printer/bookseller from manufacture towards the wider dissemination of his products, and the publishing operation began to grow up independent of the manufacturing process until it achieved the commercial separation of function which has lasted through this century. It is a wry thought that the economic conditions of today are causing a progressive reduction now in the number of distributive outlets available for books, and a greater concentration by publishers on methods of selling, or at any rate of sales stimulus, direct to potential buyers. But the geometric figure thus described is more of a spiral through time than a circle.

THE COMPONENTS OF THE INDUSTRY

There are five principal component members of the book industry: the author, the publisher, the printer, the bookseller, and—justifiably now—the librarian. Their parts will be described in turn.

The author

Although all the five people mentioned above are *sine qua non* to the communication of information through the book form, some are perhaps less '*sine*' than others. The author, as the originator of the matter to be communicated, is not among them. Without him, or his substitute, there is indeed nothing.

Types of authorship correspond, obviously, to the different types of book which are written, but there are other ways of categorising authors. The easiest distinction to be made is between the professional and the non-professional author. The former makes a living exclusively, or predominantly, from his writing, but the work which he does may be specialised or general. He may concentrate on one type of work, or one subject field, or he may be a 'journeyman' writer, perhaps a novelist primarily, who knows that novels will not by themselves earn his bread, and who therefore writes general non-fiction—travel books, histories, biographies—and is willing to accept specialist commissions, such as the writing of company histories, advertisement brochures, indeed any kind of written material, not excluding more speculative but potentially more profitable forms such as filmscripts, television plays and the like.

Throughout the present century the novel has held its status as the most artistically distinguished form of writing (poetry excluded) because of the exact synthesis of creativity and professional craftsmanship which is necessary to achieve the highest standard of the form. Serious fiction—serious, that is, in intent if not necessarily in substance—is also among the worst paid forms of writing, and there can be few professional writers of it who do not also engage in other literary forms.

There is also the argument common today that the novel is dying, or dead—that its potential has been fully explored and exposed in its long and diverse development since the pioneering eighteenth-century days of Samuel Richardson and Henry Fielding. That the point should be raised about the most prevalent modern form of the age-old art of story-telling reflects, of course, on the form, rather than on the art itself.

Julian Mitchell, the novelist, was quoted in *The Times* in 1968 as saying: 'What the novel has left is psychological . . . if I want to tell a story, I'd rather do it direct for film or television, which establishes immediately what a novel takes pages to do.' The remark illustrates a growing trend among professional writers to diversify their talents into media other than the book, no less than into subjects other than their chosen preferences.

A leader in *The Times* on 1st January, 1966 drew attention to the steadily declining output of new fiction from publishers and the risk that unknown novelists of originality might find it increasingly difficult to publish their work. This was answered, in correspondence, by a publisher who suggested that fewer authors are now tempted to write fiction because of higher earnings obtainable in other fields of writing, and who claimed that nevertheless no novel of genuine literary quality would fail to find a publisher. But this statement, and the subsequent correspondence which it provoked in *The Times*, inevitably implies that imaginative work may continue to appear in future more through deliberate maintenance of the desired aesthetic standards of publishers than because any large section of the public— borrowers or buyers—is waiting to welcome it. The firm of Blond is planning to issue in 1972 a part of its fiction list in the form of lithographed typescripts at 50p or so per book, a revealing indication of the inroads made into fiction buying by current price levels for conventionally produced books.

John Winton, himself a 'journeyman' writer, told an author/librarian conference in 1968 of the way in which he and his literary agent collaborate to provide routine writing commissions to augment his income as a novelist. He perhaps, as a 'popular' novelist, falls some way in type between the wholly 'serious' novelist (Graham Greene, Patrick White, Richard Hughes, and many others of lesser renown and sometimes greater tenacity of literary purpose), and the 'romantic' novelist (Barbara Cartland, Charity Blackstock and others) who produce 'pot-boilers'—stock-situation, formula stories with no pretensions to artistic achievement or novelty of style, which nevertheless enjoy tremendous support among less intellectually discerning readers. Yet all these writers are professionals, practising a craft in which they have skill and experience, whether their motives for writing any particular book be principally commercial or aesthetic.

The non-professional writer, on the other hand, may be a sparetime novelist (though 'non-professional' only on that account, not through any lack of serious purpose or assiduity of work—Anthony Trollope was undoubtedly a 'professional' writer, while in full-time employment as a senior government official), or a teacher who writes textbooks, or a person with a special interest (a hobby, perhaps) who can write a capable book or series of books about it.

Non-professional in another sense also is the author who is not really an author—the sporting personality who gives his name to a 'ghosted' autobiography, or the celebrated academic shown as 'editor' of a lavish coffee-table confection put together entirely in the publisher's office, whose name and brief preface represent an imprimatur of marketable quality rather than an acknowledgement of intrinsic authorship.

In modern times, the public has invariably attached an aura of glamour to an author (perhaps to compensate for its general reluctance to buy his books and gain him a living). The aura remains today, expanded to embrace journalists and critics, and the status of a writer in society, especially a professional writer, is high, although his earnings remain, on average, modest, journalists sometimes excepted. The top-selling writers can make a lot of money, but they are few, whether novelists or textbook authors, and a survey for the Society of Authors in 1965 suggested that in fact the average earnings from writing of more than 1000 of published and publishable book-authors interviewed in Britain were less than £6 per week.

The proposal for establishing a public lending right, first made by John Brophy in 1951 and developed as a minor *cause célèbre* during the sixties, to give authors a payment for public library loans of their books, recognises both this and the extent to which novels and general non-fiction are increasingly dependent upon public library purchasing to sustain their publication at all. Michael Dempsey, then chief editor of New Authors Ltd., an innovating imprint of Hutchinson's, told the conference already referred to of two first novels published in 1967 of which the public library sales were 2050 and 1300 out of total sales respectively of 2250 and 1500 copies.

Nevertheless, it remains the case that at any moment there are thousands of people in Britain (as many as 100,000 it has been suggested) engaged in writing books, most of which will never be published. The inference is that the urge to communicate and the glamour of authorship are for very many people sufficient to outweigh the usual paucity of economic reward; and it might therefore not unfairly be asked, in the context of public lending right and other projected forms of subsidy for literature, why any man should be paid out of the public purse to pursue a career from which he cannot otherwise derive a living in the public market-place. It might also be asked what could be the eventual influence upon writers of subsidy arising from so clearly discriminating a readership as the users of public libraries, where borrowings of 'romantic' fiction far outnumber those of other types of books.

Authorship, however, does often bring ancillary rewards. For some novelists there may be television interviews, lecture fees, academic fellowships, in addition to commissions for other forms of writing. Teachers invariably write their textbooks in part because of the captive audience which they know exists, as well as the advantages, when seeking promotion, of being a published author in an educational subject.

There is no doubt that, on the one hand, in spite of the (modest) level of subsidy which does exist in one form or another for creative writing, and on the other hand because of the rapid polarisation of the public demand for books into defined areas of special interest, the role of the author is increasingly circumscribed by the requirements of the public market-place, of the use which is made of books by readers, and the reasons for which they are sought. This is a large and as yet imprecisely discernible question, but the extent to which the function of the author is changing or receding as the forms of communication change is an essential corollary of the publishing process, and is discussed, with some conclusions suggested, in Chapter 5.

The publisher

Chronologically the publisher comes second in the sequence of a book's progress from its first conception to its eventual appearance in print. He is the catalyst who draws together the contributions of author, printer and bookseller into the finished product which is eventually offered for sale.

On the face of it the publisher's role is a simple one: to accept the responsibility for publication of an author's work, to control and pay for its translation into printed and bound book form, and to arrange for its sale to the market through whatever commercial processes may be appropriate. Each one of the contributors mentioned deals directly and only with the publisher; thus the author has no formal contact with the printer or the bookseller, nor they with him or with each other. The publisher takes the capital investment risk of the publication entirely on his own shoulders, and he pays each of the other contributors for their work—the printer a fixed sum for the job, and the author and bookseller a percentage of the income from sales. No further elaboration is needed at this point of this cycle of activity, since the publisher's function forms the subject of the next two chapters.

The manufacturers

There are two people primarily responsible for the physical manufacture of a book—the printer and the binder. In addition, contributions are made by the paper supplier, the graphic designer and/or illustrator, and the blockmaker.

The PRINTER is contracted by the publisher to set up type for and to print the book to the publisher's design and specification, either by letterpress (in which metal type is first cast and made up into pages and then impressed upon the paper) or by lithography (in which prepared copy is photographed and the image transferred to a series of contiguous rollers, from the last of which it is printed onto the paper).

The BINDER binds up the flat sheets which the printer has supplied, either in paper covers or board cases, by first folding the sheets, then collating the sections of the book into the correct order, sewing and gluing the sections together, trimming them and gluing them into the cloth-covered cardboard case.

Both printer and binder receive an agreed sum of money for their work, and when they have completed each job and been paid for it, physical ownership in the prearranged number of books so produced passes entirely to the publisher.

The PAPER SUPPLIER is usually a merchant, but in some cases a publisher may buy direct from a paper manufacturer, and some printers also offer at competitive prices standard paper of their own which they have bought advantageously in large quantities from a manufacturer. The choice of the type of paper to be used in a book is, like all its other physical specifications, made by the publisher.

A graphic designer may be employed by the publisher, at a pre-arranged fee (or as a full-time employee of the firm) to design the dustjacket, and perhaps the typography and layout of the interior of the book. An illustrator may be employed to illustrate the text at a fixed fee, or sometimes, if the illustrations are an integral part of the book (as is often the case with children's books), for a royalty on sales. The designer and the illustrator present their designs first as 'roughs' for approval by the publisher, and then as 'finished artwork', precisely drawn, which can be used either for 'laying down to camera' if the printing process is lithography, or, if it is letterpress, for block-making.

The BLOCKMAKER manufactures blocks (see below, p. 128, for a description) of matter to be printed which cannot be set up in type, either photographs, drawings, or decorative matter for which no type fount exists.

The bookseller

There are three kinds of booksellers—library and educational suppliers, wholesalers and retailers—and two distinctive markets in which they operate—the U.K. and overseas.

LIBRARY SUPPLIERS concentrate on selling to institutions: libraries of all kinds, public, university, college, 'special' (i.e. industrial) and school. Most of the larger suppliers concentrate on the public-library market, selling multiple copies of staple requirements, often in specially reinforced bindings which they provide. They are allowed (or, more accurately, expected) to supply at a discount (currently 10 per cent) off the published price of each net book, to libraries which hold a 'library licence' granted by the Publishers Association. This is available to libraries which are open to public access, though there are other requirements also. The suppliers employ travellers who call on customers in advance of publication with informational and promotional material, especially jackets, obtaining orders in this way, and they are substantial buyers of certain categories of books.

WHOLESALE BOOKSELLERS, who are declining in numbers as profit margins shrink in the book industry, are like wholesalers everywhere. They buy bulk from the publisher at wholesale terms and supply retailers at standard retail terms. The method enables the retailer to order from and settle with a single supplier instead of many, as would be the case if he ordered direct from each publisher. The majority of wholesale booksales is now done by U.K. houses with retailers overseas.

The RETAIL BOOKSELLER is the prime focus of the publisher's selling operation. In my earlier book I described the publisher/bookseller situation in some detail, in terms which aroused mainly adverse comment from publishers (on the ground that I had been unfair to booksellers), and mainly favourable comment from the booksellers (on the ground that I had been only too fair to publishers). I am inclined now to moderate some of the remarks I made then (in 1965), but the main thesis holds good today: with individual exceptions, for the major part of the publishing industry's output, the present retail-trade structure is entirely inadequate to *promote* the sale of books, and far too expensive for the much more passive service which it actually renders.

It is now coming to be acknowledged in practice, as it has long been recognised, that different categories of books require to be marketed in different ways. Thus a class textbook in economics for university students cannot be promoted and sold in the same way as a romantic novel. The trouble is that the U.K. book industry does not have a formal distribution structure which can encompass the variations in marketing technique which different categories of book require. There exists a differential in terms from most publishers to their trade customers for different categories of book—educational books yield less to booksellers than, say, novels—but the industry's thinking has not gone beyond varying its terms to the same customer according to the type of book which is supplied. The main point of difference between selling a university textbook and selling a novel does not rest only on the different services rendered to the publisher in the process, but involves also the different resources required.

The emphasis in new book retailing is on 'High Street' marketing—a retail shop in a prominent thoroughfare which is designed to attract casual custom into the shop by its general appearance, and then to persuade that custom into making purchases by the desirability, in appearance and in substance, of its wares. This is satisfactory, in the book industry, for novels and general non-fiction, which are speculative in their commercial nature—that is to say, the purchaser must be persuaded, from an initial situation of presumed indifference, into making a purchase.

Educational and technical books, however, are a very different commodity from novels. They are (at present) presold by the publisher, either to the ultimate market (the students), or to its referees (the teachers) by direct promotional methods (mailing shots, catalogues, inspection copies, etc., see p. 138), and the prime function of the retailer is to act as a link in the chain of physical distribution, not as a commercial persuader. For this, no glamorous retail premises ought to be needed, no special situation, indeed no special skills. The process is mechanical, rather than coercive or creative.

I had an illustration of this myself a year or so ago, when my firm published a textbook for university students which a college lecturer informed me would be a compulsory purchase for 120 students. Advised of this, the local 'university' bookseller ordered fifty copies. My main objection was that I *knew* he needed 120 in this case (because the college's compulsion was determined), and that the result would be that two days after term began we would get an anguished telephone call to rush another 70 copies down by passenger train. So I declined the order for 50 copies, and told the bookseller if he did not order the correct amount, I would simply load up the firm's van with 120 copies, drive straight to the college and sell them myself direct to the students. He ordered 120 copies, and he sold them within a fortnight and reordered.

The fault does not lie with the bookseller personally. He runs in this case a mainly general bookshop, he has experience of students' apathy about book-buying, and he feels he has to hedge his bets. It is the structure that is wrong, for if I had carried out my threat and sold this book direct to the students, I would have been subjected to very strong pressure by other booksellers over the sale of my other publications.

Another example occurred with a friend of mine who publishes a list of special-interest books. A county town branch of a large retail bookselling chain was asked by a customer to order one of my friend's publications. The assistant concerned replied that, according to their 'list', this publisher was one with whom the retail chain 'declined to deal'. The retail chain is in fact this publisher's twelfth largest customer out of some 800 regular accounts.

One final example: one of the country's principal bookselling firms approached me with a request that my company complete their standard form showing terms available from us for different quantities of different categories of publications. I replied that I could not complete the form because we did not give discounts on our books, but discounts to our customers, which were carefully assessed on a cost/benefit basis. The bookseller replied that he had never heard of cost/benefit.

These examples perhaps illustrate the central point about the U.K. book retailing system: that in spite of the fact that the publishing industry is producing a variety of commodities as different from each other in type as chalk is from cheese, they are all forced through the same retail structure. As a result, publishers of educational and technical books, which are easy and cheap to sell (no capital investment, no risk of non-sale) because they are not stocked by retailers until demand, first stimulated by the publisher's own promotional activities, has manifested itself, are subsidising the retail sale of novels and general non-fiction books, which although they need 'High Street' retailing establishments in order to sell, cannot themselves pay the expenses of them. One of the most bizarre arguments in the (successful) defence of the Net Book Agreement in the Restrictive Practices Court in 1962 was that the abolition of publishers' fixed prices would lead to price undercutting by non-book retailers which would deprive the general bookseller of his share of the institutional market for books—which does not require retail premises to operate, but which is the business the bookseller must have in order to keep his (High Street) shop open!

The foregoing paragraphs have been phrased to illustrate some of the shortcomings of the retail bookselling structure which exists today, and which has existed with very little change for the last fifty years—in spite of the inevitable trends towards bookseller groups and chains, rather than small independent shops.

It should be said, in mitigation, that the lot of the independent bookseller is extremely hard, his profit margins are derisory, and probably non-existent if stock values are taken out of account in his balance-sheet (as for tax purposes they cannot be). But the point which both publishers and booksellers are so reluctant to admit is that if national social and economic conditions are so changed as to make a particular commercial way of life uneconomic, then it is more sensible to look openly for a substitute than to prop up an outmoded way of business life. What is needed is a realisation that 'books' are no longer a single uniform commodity, but that the term is a collective one for a wide range of very disparate commodities, which require a very different set of approaches to their marketing, according to their individual natures. The bookseller—the provider of books to their ultimate consumers—has a very significant part to play in the industry. But the quaint idea that a bookshop in every town is a desirable social asset which must be provided, willy-nilly, by the publishing industry against economic reason, may have attractive associations, but it simply will not wash in terms of economic reality.

The political argument done, it should be said that the trade norm for retail bookseller discount on general books has been for many years $33\frac{1}{3}$ per cent (now mainly 35 per cent as a result of decimalisation of the currency), that a privileged few booksellers receive an additional 5 per cent (very occasionally 10 per cent) above this, and that discounts on non-general books, and on single-copy orders normally range downwards through 30 and 25 per cent, sometimes to $16\frac{2}{3}$ per cent, and occasionally as low as 10 per cent.

The crucial decision for any publisher calculating the discounts he will allow to his retailers is, quite simply, what each one individually is doing for the publisher in terms of economic value which he could not obtain elsewhere, in the same volume, more cheaply. This is, in essence, cost/benefit analysis.

The librarian

Although the librarian plays no part in the publishing process, he is included here among the component members of the book industry for two reasons: first, because of the extent to which libraries, especially public libraries, effect the physical dissemination of books to the ultimate consumer of the printed word, the reading public; and secondly, because of the enormous buying power which libraries of all kinds now represent to the publishing industry.

Broadly speaking, there are three categories of library: public libraries, academic libraries and 'special' (i.e. industrial) libraries.

PUBLIC LIBRARIES, controlled by rather fewer than 500 local authorities in the U.K., and with many times that number of service points throughout the country, are perhaps the best documented from the publisher's point of view. It is unnecessary here to trace the history of the public library movement, and suffice it to say that in the century since the founding of the (U.K.) Library Association and its incorporation twenty years later by Royal Charter, the profession as a whole has grown up on the shoulders (initially) of public librarianship to full authority as a valid and necessary part of the social and educational environment.

The struggle for public recognition of its true status was hard and long, and has really only been fully achieved in the years since the Second World War. There are many factors which have influenced the rise of professional librarianship—the growth in education, the enormous increases in scientific knowledge and activity which have generated the 'information explosion', the swift development of formal academic training for librarianship, rising national expenditure since the war on social objectives, and many others. Not the least factor crystallising these and the other influences has been the remarkable and sustained energy with which librarians themselves have promoted and proselytised their own functions and potentials. It might be possible to relate the rise of public librarianship since the war (more than 500 million loans recorded in 1969) to the corresponding decline in bookbuying by the public—the 'decline' being relative to corresponding changes in social and industrial circumstances, not absolute in terms of numbers of books sold—but the effect of public library lending on hard-cover book sales is a bone of much contention between librarians and publishers, and there is insufficient evidence to form a definite opinion.

Public libraries perform two functions for their readers—the lending function and the reference function; they lend out books for home use, and they answer reference inquiries from the public on all subjects for which reference literature exists (i.e. *all* subjects!). Debate arises among librarians whether their function is to cater only for the preferences of their readers, by concentrating on book provision which corresponds to readers' expressed tastes (e.g. mainly 'light' fiction and romance), or whether they ought to exercise some critical judgement in the selection of their stock. Practising librarians differ in their attitudes to this question, but the experience of most library users is likely to be that whatever the stock emphasis in any particular library, there will be few occasions when the user's needs, as distinct from his wants, are not satisfied.

As regards the reference services of public libraries, debate avoids moral issues, and is concerned with ensuring that in addition to a general reference service for non-specialist inquiries, each library system should endeavour to back up the resources of specialised national and industrial libraries for the benefit of specialised inquiries. Thus elaborate co-operation links exist throughout the whole library network, public and other, to collate information resources of all kinds for the benefit of any inquirer. This extraordinary breadth of service is provided almost entirely without direct charge to the inquirer.

Public library spending on books at the present time (1970) is believed to total some £15 million per year. When allowance is made for the facts that libraries offering access to the public buy at 10 per cent discount off published prices, and that total U.K. publishing turnover (1969: £70 million) is assessed after trade discount, it may be estimated that public library purchases account for about 15 to 20 per cent of all U.K. book purchasing (by value). Since public libraries almost never buy paperback books (which accounted for £7 million of the U.K. total sales in 1969) it is reasonable to conclude that library purchasing of hardcover books represents not less than 20 per cent of total sales by value—a dominant position indeed.

If public librarianship, although controlled by autonomous local authorities, nevertheless offers a truly 'national' service, ACADEMIC LIBRARIES can be regarded in the same light only by their deliberate efforts to create a uniformity of purpose and performance over the whole educational scene. Academic libraries are, of course, the libraries of individual educational institutions—universities, technical colleges, schools—though the only common feature of such widely disparate services is the fact that their purpose is to support an educational objective. For this reason, the function of academic libraries is reference rather than lending. Few university libraries stock multiple copies of textbooks which students are expected to buy for themselves; they provide instead an enormous range of reference material ancillary to the main course textbooks, with heavy concentration on periodicals and non-book materials. In school libraries, lending to pupils is more common, and the stock is not exclusively (or indeed mainly) of educational materials in the strict sense.

A SPECIAL LIBRARY, an imprecise designation, has been defined by one authority as 'an information facility designed to provide access to specialised information and placed within the range of and addressed to meet the needs of special clientèle'. It is perhaps not necessary for a publisher to be quite so cautiously general, and we may say that for practical purposes a 'special' library is a library within an industrial or commercial organisation, or an independent body such as a trade association; it is intended for the use of its own organisation, though many special libraries practice co-operation, led particularly by the national special libraries (notably the National Lending Library for Science & Technology, and the various libraries of national bodies such as, for example, the U.K. Atomic Energy Authority).

Special libraries are regarded in the library profession as the biggest growth area for the future. The expansion of scientific research and of industrial and commercial activity is generating a vast amount of information which must be stored and controlled. In this context, two principal differences emerge between special libraries and other libraries; first, they are concerned primarily with immediate information—with non-book materials, patents, research reports, documents (and a new branch of librarianship, called 'documentation' is now maturing, with its own professional institute of 'documentalists'), rather than with books, which are regarded as objects of record; secondly, they must exercise a far more active function than public libraries, at least, in disseminating information to members of their organisations to whom it may be relevant. Thus almost all special libraries of any size operate some form of 'current awareness' system by which they actively take information to the user, instead of waiting for him to come and ask for it.

These two factors have necessitated greater use of data systems of information storage and retrieval, using specially developed indexing languages and methods, than has so far been found necessary in libraries mainly concerned with book loans and 'passive' reference service.

It should be added that these brief notes are not intended as definitive summaries of the functions of different types of library but to give publishers an outline of the sort of book provision made by different libraries. Thus, for example, the university library can be seen from the above not to merit the despatch of 'inspection copies' of potential class textbooks.

These are three quite distinct strains of library development out of the common root of a central depository for the materials of communication. It is impossible to give even approximate figures for the total expenditure on books made by academic and special libraries. Some figures can be obtained (for example, spending by the university libraries), but if it were said that the total expenditure on books of all libraries in the U.K. represented 50 per cent (or 70 per cent, or 30 per cent) of publishers' total sales, so precise a statement could always be challenged in debate.

What is necessary for publishers to remember is that the library profession as a whole is a highly sophisticated and very well-integrated network of communications; that the differences between the three strains of it enumerated above are of major relevance to any book publishing programme; and that the whole profession's purchasing power in relation to total book sales is prodigious and cannot fail to increase in proportion to the growth of national income in the future.

Thus the chronological progress of a book from concept to publication can be seen in a very simple diagram:

Author → Publisher → Bookseller → Librarian
⟍Other customers:
(a) private
(b) institutional

Let us now, therefore, examine the nature and status of the product which performs this progress.

THE BOOK

The 'multiple-copy' book was the first progeny of the fifteenth-century invention of the mechanical printing press. The 'mass-readership' book (a distinction principally of distributive power) came later, in the nineteenth century. It was then, and at the time of its origin, the most effective means of publicly disseminating the communication of sustained thought or argument, and in this sense, the book is perhaps an accidental phenomenon, in that it was invented before the advent of electronic forms of communication.

During the long period of its dominance as a medium of communication it has gradually gained a cultural significance as a *form*, not just for its content. This is odd, in the multi-media age, but was perhaps less so in days before mass-circulation newspapers and periodicals, radio and television.

Looked at objectively, a book consists of a number of sheets of paper, gathered in prearranged sequence and placed for protection between boards, on which print has been placed in an order requiring its assimilation from left to right, from the top of each page downwards, beginning at the front and terminating at the back. In recent times the package has been wrapped in a paper dustjacket, initially to protect it from 'dust' (and to hide the gradual deterioration in aesthetic quality of the binding), and latterly to provide customer-attraction.

The print which appears on each page is a representation in universally accepted symbols of a concept or series of concepts. It is thus as communication *two stages removed* from the original concept, and this is very important. The first stage is the translation of the concept by the communicator into symbols (words and word-groups); the second stage is the reinterpretation of those symbols by the recipient into his own concept. The variations between the two concepts thus originated and received may therefore be considerable.

In referring to the cultural significance attached to the book form, I do not mean the aesthetic qualities which may be devoted to its physical presentation—elaborate typography, or decorative binding. This is *dressage* of the product, usually for commercial motives. I refer rather to the almost spiritual aura which has been held to surround the idea of a 'book'. Mundane examples of this can be found, for example, in the trade slogans—'Books are *different*' (from pots and pans, etc.), 'Literature is the hallmark of culture' (they mean *book* literature), and so on—or in the social distinctions which mark out a family which possesses no books as of lower *class* (not necessarily lower intellect) than one with its own library. The aura is hard to pin down in precise phraseology, but even today there exist large sections of the population, at all levels, which believe that 'books' are somehow distinctive of something, out of the ordinary by reason of their nature rather than their content. It is because of this that a (comparatively) massive book industry still continues to exist in competition with the newer media.

Of course it is true that the form which is print influences the content of the communication; this has, in effect, just been argued. Even more there are certain communications in which the use of print is intended as an integral part of the communication itself—poems for example, where the text wanders about the page in some graphic arabesque prescribed by the author as representing part of what he wants to say—just as dustbin lids are occasionally bolted onto bits of painted wood to form works of art. I invariably find these dustbin lids rather attractive to look at (the poems usually less so), but their use and effect as part of an artist's collage are not themselves a justification for the maintenance of the waste-disposal industry. They are a spin-off.

It really is essential that publishers, and all the other members of the book industry, should ignore the 'spiritual' considerations attaching to books, and should go back simply to first base-function. The questions to be asked by anyone approaching books from the professional or commercial standpoint are: 'What do books do?', and 'How well do they do it?'

What do books do?

Well, of course, they collate into a physically convenient and durable package, in an easily assimilable medium (print), the substance of communication. They not only make available the information they contain; they also store it until it is required. They are as objects generally pleasant to handle, and are considered domestically decorative. They are comparatively easy to obtain, and the range of their (cumulative) content is almost unlimited. They are a traditional and universally known form of communication. It is difficult to extend the list much further without falling into propagandist declarations like 'books are educational' (they are not—it is their substance which is, or can be), or such meaningless slogans as 'books are A Good Thing'. In terms which eschew subjective preference in favour of plain fact, the only thing which books actually 'do' is encapsulate communication.

How well do they do it?

This is a relative question, the terms 'well', or 'efficiently', or 'cheaply' implying comparison. Consideration must be given, for each of four general categories of book, to three factors:

1. the suitability of the book form for conveying communication in comparison with competing media;
2. the efficiency of distribution;
3. the price of books in relation to value.

The four general categories of book by type of content are:
    (a) fiction;
    (b) general non-fiction;
    (c) specialist non-fiction;
    (d) educational.

The first two of these are similar in purpose; that is to say, novels, biographies, travel-books and the like are primarily intended for the reader's entertainment, rather than his improvement. As products for marketing they are speculative, in that they have no group of potential customers which can be defined by any attribute except literacy, and they most often are subject to impulse-purchase instead of need-purchase. This random demand is backed to a growing extent (see earlier, p. 14) by public library purchasing in these fields, which is conducted according to a positive acquisition policy and is therefore more determinable by the publisher. It is known that X public library will automatically buy one or more copies of a new novel by Graham Greene; it is not known that a private customer in a book-shop will do so, even if he is a regular bookbuyer and a regular buyer of Graham Greene novels.

FICTION and GENERAL NON-FICTION. Random-purchase books (as these two categories may be called) depend for their sales (the numbers of which are one measure of a book's success in communication) on certain factors: the notification (by exposure of the product) of potential buyers, the existence of a clientèle committed to the activity of reading printed material, the price of the book—both in cost absolutely, and in relation to the value which it represents to the buyer. The importance of these factors in making a sale other than to the library market is total. For the other types of book mentioned—specialist non-fiction and educational books—the significance of these same factors is always only partial, because other motives inevitably inform a decision whether to purchase them.

It may also be argued that maximum dissemination of a communication is not necessarily a measure of the success of the form in which the communication is transmitted. It may be the author's preference that his work should reach an intended few, rather than a general majority; but this is not likely to be so with the authors of 'entertainment' books. ('Entertainment' is used here, obviously, in a very loose sense.)

Notification to the public of a book's existence is carried out through numerous channels, from the formality of the *British National Bibliography* entry to press reviews and advertisements. But from the point of view of the publisher's marketing policy (as distinct from the universal publishing habit of always keeping your fingers crossed), it means exposure of the product before the customer, i.e. a place on the retail bookshop's shelves or tables. The restrictions on optimum exposure contained in this are, firstly, the vast number of new books being published all the time (without equivalent deaths among the old ones), which makes it physically impossible for any bookshop to ensure even bibliographical control of the output, let alone stock and display every title, and the declining number of bookshops large enough and profitable enough to stock even a representative range of new books, in a trade environment in which any extension of consumer-marketing of books outside the retail books is fiercely resisted, even to the exclusion of direct sales by a publisher to an inquiring customer.

The general exposure of books is obtained in one other way—by their availability in public libraries but, as has been said, the influence of free lending upon private book purchasing is still only a matter of opinion. It seems likely that the nature of the 'entertainment' class of book which we are discussing, allied to its present price levels, makes library availability a disincentive to buy.

The price of a book may be examined in two ways: as an absolute (just the number of pence which it costs), or as a relative (those pence in relation to the cost of production, the cost of other similar products of comparable purpose, the amount of money possessed by the prospective purchasers, and so on).

Just taking the number of pence, it appears from statistics which are regularly published in *The Bookseller*, that the average price of a book published in 1955 was some 15*s.* 6*d.* and in 1967 37*s.*, a rate of increase of 140 per cent over a dozen years. Taking price as a relative in the same period, average weekly industrial wage rates rose by 83 per cent, and gross national product by 93 per cent. A London theatre seat rose by 130 per cent, the index of retail prices by 42 per cent. Spending on radio and television licences per head of population rose by 167 per cent. The purpose of giving these figures is not to draw conclusions from them here—that is done in Chapter 5—but to isolate the factors by which the efficiency of the book as a medium of communication must be judged. Upon its efficiency depends its future.

And it is the price of a book, viewed in relation to other factors, which most directly leads to the question of competition. To what extent, and why, are other media of communication preferred to the book form? The other media which exist are, effectively, the press (newspapers and magazines), and the audio-visual media (cinema, radio and television).

The press is not a direct competitor with the book form. It purveys largely different types of communication to that contained in books, even though there is overlapping, as when, for example, a book is serialised in a newspaper or magazine. But in general, people do not read newspapers and magazines *instead* of books; one is not seen as a substitute for the other. Indeed the press, like the book industry, is fighting the same war with the real competitor to the printed word— television—and the indications are that it is losing slowly. Forward planning departments in press combines are increasingly forecasting the decline and disappearance of multi-copy printed media (not necessarily of print). For several years now, Tokyo has had a system enabling the reader to 'dial' his newspaper from a central transmitter onto his own television screen at home.

The influences of television as a medium which act against the book are two: first, it provides in visual form much the same diet as is contained in the random-purchase books we have been discussing; secondly, for the long term, its pervasiveness and its passivity of intellectual assimilation are giving it preference for the public over the printed word. The double barrier in the printed word between communicator and recipient has been mentioned—from concept to print and from print back to concept. Visual communication has only one of these barriers, concept into image, and in many instances no barrier at all because the image is itself the communication (for example, the face of an actor on the screen, versus the written description in a book of the character portrayed). It has also a range of concept expression which is not confined to the reinterpretive powers of the recipient's imagination.

Thus the superiority in public appeal of television over the book as a medium of entertainment lies in its speed and variety of communication through the sensory processes of the recipient, when contrasted with the tortuous progress through the processes of the intellect which the printed word must make.

This superiority is not absolute. Television and reading still stand to some degree side by side in communications. A television serial of *The Forsyte Saga* prompts enormous sales of the paperback editions of the book. But the balance is swinging down slowly in favour of visual communication, and it must be remembered that children born today will take that balance as they find it when they join the communications process. The attitudes of everyone over 40 today were formed in a childhood when television did not exist.

SPECIALIST NON-FICTION: this category of book enjoys an immediate commercial advantage over the random-purchase book. It is speculative to nothing like the same extent, for it emerges largely in response to market demand, instead of having to create it. The category covers books about individual hobbies, leisure activities for the reader to undertake, and represents those books intended neither to 'entertain', nor to 'educate', but to 'instruct'. There are enormous specialist publishing lists being developed to cater for special interests —medal collecting, car repair, rose-growing, to name only a few. The more specialised the interest, the less speculative the venture, because the potential clientèle is more easily identifiable and more accessible. Thus a book on rose-growing might normally be at the speculative end of the specialised non-fiction spectrum; if, however, it is written for and published by a society of rose-growers for its own membership, it moves to the other end of the spectrum as a venture for which market accessibility, demand, requirement of content and price can be carefully calculated in advance.

Exposure is principally by direct notification of a known clientèle, with retail bookshop display lending weight according to the degree of specialisation of the subject. In highly specialist subject fields there exist also specialist retailers who may perform the notification function via their own mailing lists, in effect on the publisher's behalf. Exposure, therefore, for this category of books tends to be good.

Price, too, is far less of a limiting factor than it is with general trade books. Publishers' margins can be higher both through flexibility of pricing (either you want a book about nineteenth-century campaign medals, or you do not), and by lesser costs both of obtaining access to the known clientèle, and consequent upon more precisely estimated print runs.

In addition, there is little competition from other media. Television coverage of a special subject interest is likely to be ancillary to the subject literature in book form. The nature of special subject interest is that information about it is primarily required as a matter of record —a function which the book form is extremely well qualified to fulfil. For a subject specialist of the kind we are discussing, the subject literature is a part of the total communication which he receives, but a part which cannot be replaced adequately by media known at present, though visual forms (through such processes as electronic video recording—EVR) may make substantial inroads in the future into the dominance of the specialist non-fiction book form.

EDUCATIONAL BOOKS. Educational books, as a category, are here taken to be those which are used in association with formal teaching programmes, in universities, colleges, schools, either directly as class texts or as supplementary to the main courses. The distinction narrows between supplementary texts and the previous category of specialised non-fiction, for in many educational subjects, books in the latter category may be used as supplementary texts. (The categories which have been used throughout this discussion are *of* content, *by* marketing differences for the publisher.) We are therefore really concerned now with books which are primarily published for education.

Exposure takes place directly from the publisher to the consumer, the teachers and the students. Many textbooks are written and published in response to a specific demand from consumers. None appear without some prior reference to the consumers' needs—the opposite of the case with random-purchase books.

As a result, the role of the retail bookseller loses any characteristic of sales-promotion or the stimulation of demand. The retailer (or the wholesale supplier to education authorities) becomes physical distributor only of books which have been, in effect, presold by the publisher to his potential customers, the students, through the recommendations of their teachers. Exposure is therefore comparatively easy and efficient, though that does not mean that every pre-sale is completed by the commercial exchange of book for money. Whether a student actually buys an officially recommended textbook still depends on price and the weight of the recommendation. It is the case that student buying of educational books is very low, both in relation to the requirements of their course, and in the proportion of educational grant money provided for books which is so spent (some 20 per cent of the latter, a survey revealed a few years ago.)

Price is a very important factor in student buying, because although borrowing cannot be adequately substituted for buying since academic libraries seldom stock course textbooks in multiples, students do not have much money and textbooks are not cheap. Hence the increasing attempts by publishers to issue proved textbooks in paperback editions, at prices which reflect some saving on materials and fairly accurate calculation of demand, but which are not often significant reductions from the hardcover price in the way of random purchase paperbacks (see below, p. 27). Pricing policy for textbooks can be a 'vicious circle', for students will not buy them unless they are cheap, and they cannot be cheap unless all students buy them so that the exact foreknowledge of demand can reduce costs.

The competition which educational books encounter is not primarily, or even significantly yet, from television and other audio-visual media. The latter are coming into increasing use in lecture-halls and classrooms, as will be discussed in Chapter 5, but other non-book materials are the main competitors to textbooks—individual teaching notes, journal articles, reports, abstracts, and even practical work.

It has been observed that the book is an excellent form of record, and it is becoming widely accepted that this is the function to which textbooks should be confined—a synthesis of knowledge from disparate sources which can provide or support the central structure of an educational course, but is no longer the prime direct teaching aid. This development has been more rapid in scientific fields where the pace of research and the expansion of knowledge is too swift for the book to remain a viable form of communication. It is paralleled to some degree in the humanities by the similar use of non-book materials, not because of their immediacy so much as the broader-based teaching and learning methods which they allow—the study of history, for example, by reference to original documents, by models of houses and costume and so forth.

A take-over of educational method by technology is some way off yet, but the first step towards it has been taken in the relegation of the educational book form to status of record, not instigator, of knowledge.

PAPERBACKS. Paperbacks have hardly been discussed at all in this section concerned with the book form, because a paperback remains an example of the book form which differs only from the hardcover book as a product in the strength and quality of the materials of which it is made, and in its price.

Price is one of the three determinants discussed of the efficiency of the form, and is significant only in relation to the category of random-purchase books as far as paperbacks versus hardbacks is concerned. Its relevance to the publisher is circumscribed by the fact that no firm has so far succeeded consistently in marketing successfully long-run, low-priced novels or general books in paper covers unless they have first been issued in hardcovers. In addition, libraries decline to buy paperback editions because of destructibility, though it may be inquired whether a hardcover edition at £1.75 really has a library usage life of seven times the 25p paperback edition.

In any event, in the absence of any significant level of first publication of random-purchase books as low-price paperbacks, it cannot be assessed whether the determinant of price could be mitigated by first-instance paperbacking, resulting in more widespread purchasing.

As far as educational paperbacks are concerned, the distinction between them and hardcover editions is a different one, paper covers being a cost-saving device which does not result in striking price differentials between the two editions. The market for educational books is not capable of expansion beyond the total of students in any discipline by reason of reduced prices or alterations of format, and the object of paperback textbooks is to capture a greater proportion of the known and fixed market by a price reduction which actually increases the publisher's total sales revenue from the book. For example, a publisher may make a profit of £100 out of selling 50 hardcover textbooks at £4 to a potential market of 100 students. More desirably, he may make a profit of £150 out of selling 100 paperbacks of the same book at £2.75, but the potential market still remains at

100 students, so from £4 down to £2.75 would be the highest reduction he can make commensurate with his desired increase in profit.

In 'true' paperback publishing—random-purchase books—the hardcover edition of a novel is 2500 copies at £1.25, and the paperback edition 25,000 copies at 25p—ten times the print-order, one-fifth of the price.

This introduction to the component members of the book industry and the product with which they are concerned was intended to be descriptive rather than speculative. In Chapter 5 the situation described here will be analysed more closely, with particular emphasis on the status of the book in terms of acceptability by the public, and the competition of visual media of communication, and some possible trends in book publishing for the future will be suggested.

In the intervening chapters, we examine in some detail the practicalities of book publishing—first the publishing operation as a whole, with some discussion of the role of the small firm in the overall scene, followed by two chapters on method, financial and operational.

CHAPTER 2

THE PUBLISHING OPERATION

WE HAVE seen that the publisher is situated towards the middle of a book's physical progression from idea to finished product, and that from this situation he is the effective controller of that progression. In this chapter we shall consider the general administrative structure necessary to establish and conduct control.

First of all we must look briefly at the industrial environment of a 'developed' or technologically advanced country such as the U.K.

The Western world operates 'capitalist' economies. The economy and its form is the crux of any society, for it is the sphere of action which generates the dominating influences and characteristics of the society —employment, wealth (both national and personal), the shape of the law. All the manifestations of a society flow eventually from its macro-economic form.

The principal feature of capitalism as a system, and as opposed only to communism, is that private or corporate wealth—the value set upon or accruing from production and services—is required to be self-generating, not externally bestowed. The corollary of this is that wealth so generated accrues to the possession or benefit of the person or body who generates it. Under communism, control of industrial production lies with and wealth accrues to the society as a whole, whose authorised representatives exercise and distribute it according to criteria other than the automatic generation of further wealth, or the personal enrichment of individual members of society.

In practice, most Western countries, as everyone knows, operate a 'mixed-economy' system, which lies between 'pure' capitalism and

28

'pure' communism—that is to say, their governments appropriate a varying proportion of the gross national product, which they apply in various directions for the benefit of the community as a whole or identifiable sections of it—national health and social security services, national defence, and so on—but without seeking control of the means of production, a decisive determinant of a communist society. The extent of this appropriation, coupled with government's intervention in industrial operation on grounds of public interest, determines the degree of 'socialism' of each society—the greater the national appropriation, the more 'socialist' the society; the less the appropriation from the individual generator of wealth, the more 'capitalist'. These terms are used, of course, in an economic, not a political sense. In a phrase, the form of the industrial system denotes the *economic* colour of a society; the use actually made of that system denotes its *political* colour.

Britain is now primarily an economically socialist country, which accepts the need for a range of government control over the country's wealth that goes far beyond a basic 'membership of society' fee levied on individuals to pay for simple collective benefit. First of all, external economic management—a country's trade with other nations, is entirely the concern of its government, the purpose of which between countries of non-antagonistic political systems is to maintain equilibrium in external trade—as near as possible an exact balance between import and export. This reflects back to the home industrial environment through methods such as 'demand' management—the control of consumption, credit, stimulation of export sales, and so on.

External economic management is the principal influencing factor on internal economics. It is worth remarking that the neurotic British concern with the 'balance of payments' crises of 1964–9 developed because of the crises; it does not mean that the balance of payments is only important or an influencing factor of the internal economy in cycles of adverse trade. Its influence is equally decisive for external surplus countries, as the German efforts to reduce their surplus in recent years by acting *against* the export industry have shown.

Within the limits imposed by external trade, therefore, governments may determine the level of economic socialism by which they are able to operate the internal economy of a country. (The only external example of economic socialism—the absence or mitigation of a profit motive—lies in the 'aid' given by advanced nations to under-developed ones. It is not apparent that the communist countries are markedly less 'capitalist' in their 'aid' policies than the western world!)

The socialism of national economic policy is clearly of crucial importance to industry, for it determines in practice the extent of taxation, and the extent of government intervention in particular industries for motives which may or may not involve the enhancement of profit.

Profit is, of course, the surplus of revenue over expenditure after all charges (including taxation), which is available in a form for the dis-cretionary use (withdrawal or reinvestment) of the firm's owners. Company taxation (corporation taxes, payroll taxes, purchase taxes, transport taxes—there are nearly twenty different types of direct or indirect levy in the U.K. today) is a major determinant, after trading, of net profit. It is also argued by some that personal taxes levied upon the workforce may influence its productivity—that low tax on earn-ings is an incentive to work harder, high tax a disincentive.

Government intervention in an industry may take place with the economic motive of rationalising a number of wastefully disparate industrial units into a large group with greater collective resource for, say, international marketing; or with a social motive, such as the control or reduction of prices charged for universal services (trans-port nationalisation) and the expansion of their technological develop-ment (postal and telecommunications services), or simply to keep up employment in 'depressed' areas (coal mines).

Although it suffers from, or contributes equally with the rest of industry to, general taxation, publishing has not so far been thought a sufficiently significant industry to warrant government intervention in the form of obvious control. Interference with the news press is inhibited by the political implications of totalitarianism. Book pub-lishing is pretty small beer. But taxation is the second factor, after profit, which must determine the structure of a publishing business, and it influences particularly the first decision for a new or existing enterprise—the corporate form which it should take.

COMPANY STRUCTURE

There are effectively four different types of corporate structure commonly recognised in Britain under the various Companies Acts for the purpose of trade—the sole trader, the partnership, the company limited by shares, the company limited by guarantee. Numerically, the company limited by shares is the most common, but each type will be discussed in turn.

Sole trader

Subject to the general law of the land, anyone may engage in legitimate trade with anyone else. Without corporate status, however, a trader is personally liable in full for the debts and obligations which he incurs in the course of trade. This is specially important in any kind of manufacturing business where the trader has to purchase either a product, or capital equipment with which to manufacture one, before he begins trading. The inability of a book publisher to pay for the printing and binding costs of an edition out of sales revenue from the book leaves him, if unincorporated, personally liable in law down to his bootlaces, with the ultimate risk in default of being declared bankrupt by the court, which carries numerous practical disadvantages until the bankruptcy has been discharged. This is the principal argument against carrying on a publishing business as a 'sole trader'. A lesser argument is that 'Ltd.' accords more status in the context of business relations with suppliers, not least because it presupposes the existence of some capital behind the enterprise, however small; though it is interesting that most small publishing firms which are incorporated drop the 'Ltd.' from their publishing imprint on their books, to establish a more personal image for the business. Thus, for example, the publications of André Deutsch Ltd. carry the imprint 'André Deutsch' on their title-pages, though, as is customary, the firm's full name and address are given in the 'colophon' on the reverse of the title-page. A sole trader would normally register himself as such with the Registrar of Business Names, in order to secure some measure of protection against a competitor later adopting the same or similar style and title.

Partnership

This creates a formal legal situation, in which a deed of partnership must be drawn up declaring the names and business intentions
of the partners in the enterprise. It involves the partners in personal
liability in the same way as sole trading, but, equally, for a small
business it carries the tax advantage that all profits are assessable for
tax as the earned income of the partners, so that only personal taxation is levied. The discriminatory provisions of the 1965 Finance Act
against 'close' (privately owned limited liability) companies made
partnership, in an enterprise yielding profits of up to £10,000 for
each participating member, more advantageous for taxation than
limited liability, but subsequent Finance Acts have somewhat
reduced the stringency of the 1965 Act.

Company limited by shares

A limited liability company is 'limited' in its financial obligations
to the value of the shares issued in the company—its capital—and
assets. For the purposes of the law, it is an entity entirely distinct
from the persons of its members or owners, and if it fails, no penalty
beyond the amount of their shareholdings attaches to its members.
Members are, of course, personally liable for fraud or other criminal
activity in the operation of the company, and one relevant extension
of personal liability is that the principal of a publishing firm can, in
theory, be jailed for publishing a libel. It must be added that the
device of limiting liability by incorporation was intended to prevent
the undue personal hardship which could occur to private individuals
from the inadvertent failure of a business; it does not provide a
licence for corporate irresponsibility, and the law regulating the
conduct of a limited company, both in relation to its members and
those with whom it trades, is immense and complex.

A limited company may be 'public' or private. In the former the
shareholders are not restricted in their right to sell or transfer their
shares. The reverse of this provision is obligatory for a private company, which, in addition, may not have a shareholding membership
exceeding fifty.

The legal advantages of a private company are that it need have no more than two members (seven is the minimum for a public company), it need have only one director (plus a company secretary), and it is exempted from certain requirements concerning the issue of shares and the holding of statutory meetings. Practical disadvantages include the 1965 Finance Act requirements concerning the distribution of profits and disclosure of information, as well as the incidence of estate duty on the owners of a company which may, if the value of the company is high, compromise its continuance in private hands after the death of a principal shareholder.

Although it is possible for a company to begin life as a public company, it is almost always the case that it starts private, and may eventually expand to the size where 'going public' provides the owners with the opportunity of liquidating a large part of their investment, and the company with the prospect of drawing on public subscription for further development capital. Stock exchanges normally require the achievement of a certain profit level before allowing quotation of, and trading on, their floors in a company's shares. A stock-market quotation is, however, a convenience, not a legal prerequisite for going public. For most new publishing firms the corporate progress responds to practical need rather than fiscal planning: the prospective publisher incorporates his company to avoid personal liability for its debts; he forms it as a private company in order to retain for himself the benefits of its growth, and to restrict his responsibility in operating it to himself and a few other members rather than to the investing public at large; and eventually, when the size of the business justifies it, he places a proportion of the shares on the open market to encash the fruits of his development work and obtain access to public investment to finance future growth.

Company limited by guarantee

An uncommon form of incorporation, this type of company is limited to that amount of prearranged (guaranteed) contribution by each member to its assets in the event of failure. There is little significant difference in the legal requirements of such a company and those of a company limited by shares. It is also possible to register an *un*limited company, which must conform to certain provisions of the Companies Acts, but this is almost never done.

The technicalities of forming a company or drawing up a deed of partnership are entirely conventional and not particularly complicated. The would-be publisher, however, is better advised to leave them in the hands of a qualified lawyer and accountant, than to attempt to save the modest professional fee involved by arranging them himself. If it is intended to publish books under an imprint other than, or in addition to, the registered name of the company, it is worth while registering the imprint, for a nominal fee, with the Registrar of Business Names, and thereby secure priority for the imprint against subsequent users.

The formal requirements of operation of a company under the Companies Acts (annual returns, records of meetings, etc.) can be left to the advice of the publisher's lawyer and accountant. Both are essential advisers for any businessman.

RESOURCES AND THEIR DISPOSITION

It has already been argued that in the capitalist society of the Western world, wealth is required to be self-generating. In practical terms this means that the businessman, if he is to continue in business, is obliged to ensure that the total of his business income consistently exceeds the total of his business expenditure. If he does not, only government intervention on non-economic grounds will keep him afloat, and no such intervention has as yet occurred in the book-publishing industry.

It is important to keep this elementary proposition in the forefront of the publisher's preoccupations, for, in the nature of the business, it often tends to lapse. The publisher as manufacturer of a product suffers from two inherent disadvantages:

(i) His product is a low-unit price commodity of limited life-span, so that he is in fact producing as many *brand-new* products each year as he produces titles. Each book title is a new product, which means that a publisher of fifty titles a year has to go through the complete new-product-marketing process fifty times a year, and make enough profit or little enough loss out of each separate marketing process to cumulate into an overall profit at the end of a year. In this sense, a publishing firm is like a 'conglomerate', or industrial holding company, but with all its interests in one sphere—there is no diversification of products, as is the essence of conglomerates, but only a modest diversity of market area between, say, fiction-buyers and textbook buyers.

(ii) The substance of the product allows value-judgement (indeed demands it in many cases) by the publisher in its selection for publication, so that quite apart from the risk of error in estimating market potential for a book, there is often the added factor that a book may be accepted for publication on grounds other than its commercial prospects—because of its literary qualities, because it completes a subject coverage in the publisher's list, or some similar reason. To publish a book in deliberate anticipation of reduced profit or possible loss may be fair enough in the context of an overall publishing policy, but it is obviously important that it *should* be deliberate and *should* be in the context of overall policy, so that the adverse trading effect is allowed for in advance. In addition it must be acknowledged that 'loss' publishing is an abnormal occurrence subsidised by, if possible, a specific profit made elsewhere in the publishing programme, and not an automatic feature of a publishing programme. 'Prestige' (i.e. unprofitable) publishing, as has been said, is seldom the result of pre-planning.

The obligatory objective at the outset of each and every publishing programme is the maximisation of profit, superior to all other objectives within the business. When the maximum profit has been made, it can then be disposed to fulfil secondary objectives—but first it must be made.

Profit, therefore, is the only absolute criterion by which to frame the business structure, and thus to organise resources and their use.

Resources consist of capital and income, from existing (backlist) and new publications; their disposition is towards manufacturing costs, running costs, and profit (the subsequent allocation of which is discussed later in this chapter, p. 46).

Capital

The requirements and use of capital are considered in detail in Chapter 3, which is concerned with the financial planning of a publishing operation. Suffice it therefore for the moment to say that the function of capital is to buy trading capacity, either plant and equipment, finished goods, or services which promote the inflow of revenue. Its availability, from whatever source, is inevitably dependent upon the return to be obtained from it.

It is fashionable for financial commentators to observe that the publishing industry tends to be under-capitalised—that few firms have adequate capital in relation to their levels of trade. The statement bears some examination, for it is only a half-truth.

If, for example, publishing firm A is making a net profit of £5000 a year with capital of £5000, it may be valid to say either (a) that the firm is undercapitalised in comparison with GEC Ltd. which employs £320m. capital and produced in 1969 a net profit after tax of £60m.; or else (b) (the complete opposite in tone) that firm A shows a wonderful return on capital employed (100 per cent) compared with a 'blue-chip' like GEC Ltd. (only 20 per cent).

There is a further complication in the fact that it is difficult precisely to define the 'capital' employed in a publishing firm, since a large part of what is actually capital investment—namely the cost of printing and binding new books—is shown in a company's accounts not as capital but as trading expenditure on the profit and loss account. The value of stock in hand may be grossed up into the share capital before a ratio of profit to capital employed is calculated, but it would no less accurately reflect the nature of the business if current manufacturing cost were also added to capital, except for the taxation increase on the higher profit which would result. Theoretically, the option is a high profit on sales and a low return on capital employed, or vice versa—suggesting that return on capital employed is, like all investment criteria, not an absolute, but only one of several factors to consider when assessing a company or project.

The judgement of capital sufficiency for publishing, therefore, depends not on some arbitrary ratio between capital employed and sales volume, but on whether the capital employed is sufficient to enable firm A to operate at its maximum acceptable profit potential, and whether additional capital would generate greater profit, and so increase the overall rate of return on the new total of capital employed. It must be remembered that the only ways to increase the return on capital employed in publishing are either to sell more copies of the same number of books, or to increase the selling prices of the books without equally increasing costs or reducing sales (i.e. widening the margins); selling the same number of copies of additional titles on the same margins may increase the sum of the profit, but not the rate of return, since the additional titles require additional capital investment to produce.

The servicing of capital resources, therefore—their refurbishing or reappraisal, as distinct from estimates of needs or actual uses—hinges upon the maintenance or expansion of margins, and upon the increment of volume sales per title. Too often individual publishing firms in the U.K. are concerned only with maintaining turnover levels by the comparatively simple expedient of publishing more titles, on the assumption that so long as the *sum* of the profit increases, all must be well. It is a business approach of this kind which has tended to make publishing unattractive to outside industry (see Chapter 3, p. 61); the financial difficulties which can result from the excessive stockbuilding thereby promoted are perhaps interpreted by investment commentators as being due to 'under-capitalisation'. Increasing the rate of return on capital employed in publishing is only in unusual circumstances possible by the straightforward injection of more capital.

Income

Income is derived from two sources: book sales and subsidiary rights (the former is taken to incorporate sales of non-book materials as part of a publishing programme).

BOOK SALES. The majority of publishers' sales is to the distributive trade—wholesale and retail booksellers. Many publishers now find that an increasing number of sales is made direct to the customer. The trade politics on the subject of direct selling have been touched upon briefly in Chapter 1, and it is not necessary here to consider the extraordinarily complex attitudes and emotions which the question has engendered among publishers and booksellers (or such occasional inanities as the publisher who either refuses a retail sale and directs the customer to 'his nearest bookshop', or accepts the sale and hands over part of the payment to a preselected bookshop as 'discount').

The publisher's attitude towards the sale of his books should be obvious; he will sell to whoever wants his books through the most profitable and efficient medium both for obtaining an individual sale and for promoting further sales in the future. This attitude is conditioned by an overall policy of sales maximisation, and publishers therefore will not disturb a situation in which bookshops are actively promoting and selling their books for the short-term advantage of a few direct (full-price) sales of individual titles. If a bookseller cavils, however, at a publisher's acceptance of an unsolicited order accompanied by cash from a non-trade customer, he is merely wasting time on retrospective argument which would be better spent on seeking out new sales.

The situation is different where the retailer cannot or will not sell the publisher's products. I recently began publishing a list of textbooks in a new subject area which possessed little published literature. Response from the booksellers invited to help in promoting sales was derisory, on the grounds that there was 'no demand' for these books. We accordingly concentrated on creating and discovering demand by direct promotion and direct sales, with highly satisfactory results. There are, however, a number of skilled and sales-conscious booksellers engaged in the active promotion of new books. They deserve the fullest support from their supplying publishers, for the single reason that they *sell his books*.

It is essential for the publisher, whatever his subject field, to disregard the conventional division of 'trade' sales and 'non-trade' sales. The publisher has only 'customers', whether they be booksellers or not, and his business depends on the satisfaction of those customers in the broadest sense, not on his subservience to ancient trade shibboleths. The bookseller doesn't receive discount because he is a bookseller, but because he *sells* books.

SUBSIDIARY RIGHTS. The main uses which may be made of written communication other than original publication in hardcover book form give rise to the following saleable rights, some or all of which may be in the control of the originating publisher under his agreement with the author.

Paperback rights licensed to another publisher are usually sold for an advance payment against future royalties, which can vary between $7\frac{1}{2}$ per cent and $12\frac{1}{2}$ per cent of the paperback selling price. The license is usually for a fixed period (two to five years) with an agreed delay before publication of the paperback edition to allow exploitation of the hardcover market. Although some of the steam has gone out of the paperback industry in recent years, and the standard levels of advances paid are now more in line with hardcover publishers' advances, the paperback edition represents a serious encroachment into the originating publisher's market territories, and the latter therefore invariably receives a share of paperback rights income, usually 40–50 per cent. Paperback revenue is the principal source of subsidiary income for the originating publisher.

Serial rights to a newspaper or magazine for reproduction of all or part of a book, embrace several alternative 'packages'—*first* serial rights, *second* serial rights, *subsequent* serial rights (all including, if negotiated, syndication rights), *one-shot* (single extract) rights. There is a useful further distinction—second rights *before* book publication, and the same rights *after* publication, sold separately. Serial rights income seldom accrues in more than token sums to the originating publisher. The substantial amounts which newspapers sometimes pay for serialisation are increasingly accepted as the author's due.

Anthology and *quotation* rights provide a small dribble of income to publishers of appropriate source material, which is usually divided equally with the author, though the sums paid are frequently so small (one guinea is common for short extracts) that they may be hardly worth the cost of collection.

Book club rights yield a small royalty on the low price of fixed quantity book club editions. There are a number of book clubs devoted to special interest topics—science fiction, jazz music, gardening, and others, as well as general fiction. The income is small and shared with the author.

Foreign language rights may be within the originating publisher's control and he will take a percentage of income (advance against a usual royalty of 5 per cent—the foreign publisher has to pay for translation) which may vary from 10 to 50 per cent; the latter percentage is common only where the rights sold are 'vernacular' (i.e. into a second language within the publisher's English-speaking territory) rather than 'foreign'.

Broadcasting, dramatisation, film digest and *condensation* rights may occasionally produce marginal sums for the originating publisher. These lesser rights are fully explained in several current handbooks of publishing.

For publishers of general trade books, subsidiary rights income, mainly from paperback sales, can form a valuable and significant contribution to revenue. Although paperback publishers are moving steadily outwards from their earlier concentration on fiction, and now produce general non-fiction and some technical titles, there is a corresponding tendency on their part to commission many of these books direct from an author for original publication in paperback; hardcover rights for a 'library' edition may then be sold to a hardcover publisher, in a reversal of the usual sequence. Educational paperbacks are more often than not original commissions as part of a planned educational series. Equally, publishers of hardcover educational books usually issue their own paperback editions if desirable, instead of selling the rights—a logical attitude, since they already have both outlets and reputation in their own educational fields (see Chapter 1, p. 26).

EXPENDITURE

As is described more fully in Chapter 3, the publisher's expenditure is conveniently divided into (i) the cost of making the product (manufacturing costs) and (ii) the cost of administering the business (overhead cost).

Manufacturing costs

Normally grouped together as manufacturing costs are the physical production costs of the book and the author's royalty. Some publishers might argue that authors' royalties are more strictly running costs, both because as earnings on sales of a book they are recurrent during the book's life, not single payments, and because their sum total is not known in advance. It is, however, more convenient to regard them as manufacturing costs for two reasons: first of all they are a prior charge upon the publisher's sales revenue at a known rate, even though their total is not known in advance; and secondly, by so regarding them, they can be incorporated into the costing of a book by which the gross profit margins are calculated, so that they need not form part of the overhead budget forecasts, in which accuracy is subject to possible error.

Production costs comprise the fixed amounts payable to those participants in the book's physical manufacture who have been identified in Chapter 1—the binder, printer, paper supplier, and others. It is on the basis of these costs for the whole edition, known in advance from estimates, that the product's selling price is determined (see Chapter 3). As single sums, payable in advance of the book's sales, the production costs represent the publisher's capital investment in his product, a non-reversible outlay which secures him ownership of marketable goods.

Authors' royalties are paid on a scale which ranges between usual extremes of 5 per cent and 15 per cent of the published price of the book. The latter price is a more convenient base for calculation than the publisher's net revenue (i.e. after bookseller-discount) because of the variation in trade terms between different classes of customer, with the elaborate analysis of sales which percentages calculated upon it would require. It must be remembered that a royalty of 10 per cent really represents a charge to the publisher of some 15 per cent of his revenue after allowing standard trade terms. It is usual, therefore, for export sales at a discount of 50 per cent or more off the published

price to carry the same royalty rate as standard terms sales, but calculated on the publishers' net receipts instead of on the published
price. This allows the publisher greater flexibility in negotiating
terms—with individual overseas customers in difficult markets, or for
substantial quantities of copies.

Many author-contracts provide for a rising scale of royalty as sales
reach higher levels. My own view is that this is dangerous for the
publisher unless he can encompass the quite complex mathematics
necessary to cover the increases in his primary costing. In practice
the stages of increase often only come into effect at sales figures which
are higher than the first printing, that is, upon reprinting, and reprints are usually uneconomic anyway, and frequently excluded in
the author contract from a sliding royalty scale. Otherwise, a situation
in which a higher royalty rate comes into force at sales of 3000 copies
when the first edition is only 2500 copies might turn against the
decision to reprint at all. If reprints are specifically excluded from the
rising royalty scale, then the scale may be meaningless anyway. It's
justification can only be for large-selling authors where the doubt lies
between sales of, say, 20,000 copies or 30,000. Even there the possi-
bility of a higher royalty rate on reprint has to be taken into the
original costing.

Whatever his royalty policy, it is always useful for a publisher to
outline to his authors at the time of agreement for publication, the
costing structure on which his royalty offer is based. The author may
reasonably expect a larger share of an increased percentage profit
from extra sales of his work beyond a certain figure, but to give him
the same percentage profit on increased sales revenue merely reduces
the publisher's overall return on capital.

Advances against future royalty earnings are a traditional, but by
no means automatic part of the publishing business. They serve many
purposes. In general publishing they are often the bait by which the
publisher obtains the book. In technical publishing they may reimburse the author for expenses incurred in writing a particular work.
They may keep a novelist in bread while he writes, or simply be an
additional incentive for a busy teacher to accept a commission to
write a textbook. One important point for the publisher to consider is
that an advance of £500 paid on signature of a contract for a book to

be delivered in manuscript a year ahead, will actually cost £600 at interest rates of around 10 per cent by the time the first royalty accounting arrives after publishing, and nearer £700 if the payment is discounted at current (1970) rates of inflation.

Overheads

The costs of administering the enterprise can be grouped conveniently into four main areas, which correspond with the departmental divisions of the business—establishment, editorial, production, sales. Heads of expenditure will be enumerated in each area, but it is difficult to give valid percentages for each as a proportion of total overheads because of the variations in emphasis between departments in different kinds of publishing firms. Thus, for example, half my own staff is concerned with sales and distribution, and about one-third with editorial. In another small firm of my knowledge, two-thirds of the staff are concerned with editorial and there is no distribution and accounting overhead at all, because these functions are contracted outside the firm on a percentage-of-turnover fee, and therefore represent, for costing purposes, a prior charge on margins, not an overhead, in the same way as the author's royalty described above.

Establishment overheads are those covering the servicing of the office and/or warehouse premises and those general expenses which it would be pedantic to apportion between departments—rent, rates, heat, light, telephone, bought ledger accounting, repairs, cleaning, office stationery, insurances—as well as financing costs such as loan interest, bank charges, depreciation, legal and accountancy fees. (The main purpose of apportionment between departments is to facilitate identification and control of any increases, and if, therefore, any one department spends notably more on an establishment cost than the others—for example, sales department telephone calls overseas, or editorial expenses on legal advice—it is reasonable to charge a portion of the total to that department for comparative purposes in subsequent years.)

Significant expenses such as rents (it is generally agreed that it is always more advantageous to dispose of freehold office premises on 'leaseback' if the business has any true profit potential at all) may vary considerably in different parts of the country, but on the assumption that the premises required will relate to the scale of the business without enormous variations in the ratio between rent payable and sales revenue, it may be suggested that a median expenditure on establishment costs would lie in the area of about 20–25 per cent of total overheads, the salaries of bought ledger and general administrative staff included.

EDITORIAL overheads ought, without the allocation of parts of the establishment costs, such as rent and telephone, to be lower. They are mainly incurred by the salaries of editorial staff, which are not among the highest of the publisher's staff costs, without a great deal of outside purchasing, beyond, for example, legal advice over tendentious manuscripts, and travel in search of new books. Entertainment by editors, of authors and their literary agents, is probably in some decline since the 1965 Finance Act disallowed business entertainment, other than of overseas buyers, for tax relief. It still, of course, occurs, for a single Act of Parliament does not immediately change the entrenched business customs of an industry, but will be subject to much greater financial discretion and less gastronomic impulse than used to be the case. Let us argue an editorial percentage of overheads of 15–20 per cent.

PRODUCTION overheads, similarly, involve little outside purchasing. A small production staff can cope with a large number of titles, especially if the ancillary tasks of design and typography are contracted outside the firm and rank among manufacturing costs instead of as staff time on overheads. Ten to fifteen per cent of total overheads is suggested.

The percentages allocated above under broad headings leave half the total overhead expenses to be applied to sales. This is less disproportionate than might appear at first sight, not just because of the primary importance of the selling operation, but because of the variety of disparate activities which have to be grouped under 'sales'.

Apart from resident sales staff, the travelling representatives receive commission on revenue from their territories, allied usually to a basic salary, but the ranking of revenue for agents' commission —either 'house' representatives or independent agents overseas— varies from rep. to rep. and territory to territory, so that it is more simply treated as a staff overhead (under sales) than as a determinable prior charge on the margins.

Expense in entertaining and travel is incurred to a greater degree in pursuit of sales than in the other departments of the publishing firm, including travel overseas. But a large section of the overhead tentatively allocated to the sales function covers publicity and promotion— not only advertising, but also promotional literature, catalogues, mailing shots and the often massive costs of their despatch.

As the publishing industry comes to realise that books, as products, have to be sold, not merely displayed to the customers' passing eye on the bookseller's shelves and tables, and as the trend in materials published moves from the speculative area of fiction and general non-fiction to subject fields which cater for definable interests and endeavours, so the direction of the sales organisations moves to bring the products more aggressively to the notice of the potential customer. The retail bookshop attracts within its doors on impulse only a small number of those who actually buy books in the course of a year—far too few to make viable the extent of the book publishing now undertaken. The trend is increasingly for the publisher to make the sales approach direct to the ultimate customer, and to use the bookshop as the accessible depository in which the physical exchange of book for money occurs. This means the allocation of a constantly growing proportion of resources to catalogue production, to leaflets describing individual books or groups of books, and to the maintenance of mailing lists of recipients for this material.

My own firm which, though small, is not untypical in this respect, has swung completely in five years from a reliance on booksellers to sell its publications to a policy of direct mail, inspection and 'desk' copy distribution to potential buyers, whose orders are then serviced through the bookshops if they are so placed. We endeavour to back this by ensuring that certain bookshops carry stocks of our publications to fulfil the orders thus generated by our promotion. We are, like other publishers, greatly aided in our promotion by those booksellers who conduct their own promotional mailing operations—listing new books by subject in their own catalogues, including publishers' own leaflets in their regular mailings to customers, and, in the case of library suppliers, travelling dustjackets by their own representatives to libraries and institutions so as to secure orders in advance of publication. The value to us of the few booksellers who operate in this way is immense, and it is unlikely that we would wish to disturb our worth-while business arrangements with them. Some unconscious duplication of effort inevitably takes place, but it is not difficult to avoid on a large scale by planning promotional activities in discussion with these booksellers, and thus saving ourselves considerable postage costs. Nevertheless, my company direct-mails every year an average of one promotional shot for every £2.50 worth of gross sales revenue, and the cost to us of this part of our operation is between 5 and 10 per cent of our total overhead, excluding any allocation for the staff time involved.

It is, of course, in this context that earlier and subsequent remarks must be read about the need to treat booksellers in their individual situations as customers of the publisher, not as some collective millstone round his neck. All the comments made earlier about a decline in the publication of books saleable only by physical exposure to random purchase, about the changing nature of the book form in the communication process, and the structural inadequacy of the bookselling trade as a whole, point the publisher's need to *sell* his products to his consumers, and, like every other manufacturing industry of significance, to regard his retailers as staging posts in the line of distribution. They cannot carry the burden of initiating sales if the publisher does no more than drop the product on their shelves.

Whether, in this developing situation, book prices can continue to carry the rising costs of both an initiating sales programme by the publisher and a retail discount level which, when originally established, presupposed the onus of initiation to lie with the retailer, is another matter.

PROFIT

Profit serves three purposes: to reward the investor, either of capital or of industry; to provide resources for reinvestment to pay for expansion; to measure efficiency of operation.

The *investor's reward*, or anticipated reward, is the mainspring of the capitalist system and need not be analysed here. Without a sufficient reward—and the most common human currency for reward is still money, and not moral or spiritual satisfaction, whatever some of the instigators of taxation may claim—there is no incentive to further investment of money or effort. This incentive is no less important for the individual publisher than for the dispassionate provider of finance, for its opposite, disincentive, is not a sudden phenomenon which makes him throw in his hand on impulse, but a belief which cumulates gradually and the more irrevocably for its graduality.

The provision of resources for *reinvestment* out of profits is, in the publishing industry, a notion which pays lip service to orthodox economic theory rather than actively assisting expansion. It is repeated several times in this book both that a sizeable portion of a publisher's profit is represented by unsold stock, so that the money surplus after taxation hardly permits dramatic expansion, and that each new book is a new product requiring a new capital investment for its existence. This can be illustrated by a publisher making 15 per cent net pre-tax profit on turnover with an increased stock retention of 5 per cent. After tax he would have sufficient profit in cash (assuming no shareholders' dividend is paid) to finance approximately one new 320-page book in a 4000-copy edition for every £100,000 of his gross sales revenue. To achieve £100,000 of turnover on average new book editions of 4000 copies and with a moderately active back list, he would be publishing thirty to forty new titles per year with an average selling price of about £2 to £2.50 per title. So the expansion possible from diverting all surplus cash profit to reinvestment in standard-line publishing would be about 3–4 per cent maximum per year!

Profit as a measure of *efficiency* is perhaps neglected in publishing as a current management tool. Comparison between the results for two or more full years can provide useful general data about the nature of the publishing operation as a whole. Profit comparisons on short-term, or even title-by-title bases, on the other hand, can provide an excellent yardstick for evaluating the details of current performance, most particularly if they are made in relation to overhead expenditure.

The more I see of publishing as a business (and I refer to routine, mainstream publishing, not the spectacular and speculative ventures alternately landed with remarkable bestsellers and bizarre flops) the more firmly convinced I become that one of the most important facets of profitability is the regular and persistent attack on overheads.

Although it will be argued in Chapter 3 that each book must be costed individually, and not according to some vague general costing policy, if maximum profit is to be obtained, it nevertheless remains true that in fixing production cost margins on individual book titles, which is what costing does, comparatively little flexibility is available in terms of the effect on overall profit from a multi-title publishing programme.

Running costs are a different matter. Very considerable flexibility is available, if the profit motive is paramount, in examining detailed comparisons of out-turn over particular short-term (quarterly, even monthly) periods. The primacy of the profit motive may involve disagreeable conclusions—for example, that it is cheaper for the managing director of a small firm to spend an hour a day stuffing mailing shots into envelopes than to employ an office junior, or that a heavy-duty typewriter operated by a 16-year-old girl bashing out invoices eight hours a day from orders laboriously marked up by the sales manager represents a saving on a beautiful piece of automatic invoicing and stock-control machinery which endlessly fascinates the non-technical staff by its chattering, and its relentless churning out of pre-folded sequences of printed paper.

But the business ethic remains true. If you are in business, you are in business to make a profit, whether it be from books or badminton rackets. First *make* the profit, then spend it, if you will, on making life easier.

Individual passages in this chapter have perhaps wandered from an entirely factual exposition of publishing as an industrial activity. They have done so by design, for in the management of any enterprise it is necessary not only to grasp the technical details, but also to be able to 'think' the business, to view it in broadly industrial, not lesser, terms.

In the next section we concentrate explicitly on small publishing operations. In so far as the whole of this book is in a sense devoted to 'small' publishing operations (what publishing firm is not small by comparison with the household names of British industry? Penguin's sales revenue in 1969 was only £6m.), the caveat is the introductory contention (p. xi) that a large publishing firm is no more in essence than an amalgam of a given number of small publishing firms.

THE ROLE OF THE SMALL PUBLISHER

A small business may be so either as an end in itself which satisfies its proprietors, or it may be at the starting-point of becoming a big business. Just what constitutes a 'small' business is a matter of relative interpretation—the recent government-instituted inquiry into small businesses defined its subjects as firms with a payroll of less than 200 people, which would encompass all but a dozen or so British book-publishing firms. For the practical purposes of this discussion, a small publishing business may be defined as one in which ownership and executive control lie with only one or two persons, in which the firm really *is* the person who runs it, even though he employs other staff; a medium-sized firm has responsibility spread among a board of directors, who may or may not be owners, but still presents a 'personal' image, associated with the persons who run it; a large firm is in this sense 'depersonalised' in its management and ownership.

These groupings may be qualified by arbitrary divisions of annual sales revenue—small firm, up to £250,000 (micro-firm up to £50,000); medium-sized firm up to £750,000; large firm over £750,000. This is still very small by comparison with other areas of industry. The largest firms of all in British publishing achieve sales revenue in the range of £6–£10 m., so there is an obvious idiosyncrasy in claiming that a £750,000 firm is a 'large' one also. But the usefulness of categorising a firm as small, medium or large is limited, and the distinctions are only offered here to identify the publishers at whom this section is particularly directed; the exercise of personal control of a business is the yardstick, more than any arbitrary level of sales.

Small businesses are an important part of the national economy, responsible for a surprisingly high proportion of national exports. They range from light engineering companies with annual sales of millions of pounds, to a pair of brothers describing themselves as

'builders and decorators'. They are, as firms, either static or expan-
sionary, the former with little future in the business environment of
today, where costs and wages, the production runs necessary to
justify expensive plant, and the marketing implications of international trade, no less than taxation, are provoking that dissolution or
absorption of small units which was referred to in the introduction
to this book.

In publishing, small firms can be more evenly divided between the
static and the dynamic than in most industries, because of the comparatively low capital investment required for the manufacture of
each product, and because the pricing structure of the industry's
product is based on short runs. The qualification to this is that it is
very difficult to remain static. The inclination of the industrial
activity of book publishing is either upward (by maintaining a constant or increasing rate of new-title publishing, to add extra revenue
on to sales from a correspondingly rising back list), or downward (as
the number of new titles falls and the back list declines as editions
terminate). The number of titles published is by no means the determinant on its own of financial growth or decline. More relevant is the
gross selling price of the group of new titles published in a given
period. There is a graph illustrating this in the section of Chapter 3
devoted to management controls (Fig. 11, p. 103).

In general, therefore, most small firms which are non-dynamic
either decline or grow only very gradually (by not more than 10 per
cent, say) from year to year, and the likelihood is that any such firm is
run by a proprietor at best unwilling or at worst unable to apply the
strict criteria of profit to its operation in precedence over his own
'job-satisfaction'. Their sacrifice, in addition to profit, is of 'efficiency
satisfaction', of the knowledge that the business is operating in the
'best' manner possible according to objective standards of business
judgement.

The majority of people who start up book-publishing businesses
of their own are of the other kind—determined to succeed (by the
standard of financial growth) and indeed unable to be other than so
determined in a business as hard as publishing. Motives may be
varied, and initial objectives range from the achievement of commercial stability to the accumulation of a fortune. Because of this,

certain points should be made about the potential for growth in book publishing.

Very occasionally a publisher may come up with a completely new idea which will evolve into a massive personal fortune. The late Sir Allen Lane did it in the 1930s with Penguin paperbacks. It is possible to argue that the extent of his success was fortuitous, for it was thirty years after its inception that Penguin went public. Robert Maxwell did it in the 1950s and 1960s, with his premature recognition of the publishing potential in the post-war explosion of scientific research. Paul Hamlyn did it with cheap mass-market leisure books of high manufacturing quality; George Rainbird, like others, introduced international joint editions of coffee-table books, Gregg and others pioneered academic reprints, and Marshall-Cavendish their part-publications. Subsequent developments have revealed qualifications to all these ventures.

The important and probably prerequisite point about these dramatically successful operations is that none of them were really ideas for new *books*; they were all ideas for *marketing*, within or near the framework of the book form. This illustrates exactly the ethic from which the present work is written—the book is only a form; the publisher is selling *communication*, to which the form is incidental, not necessarily integral.

For conventional publishing based upon the book form, or, according to the above dogma, on the limited market potential and flexibility of the form which most communication permits, growth cannot often be dramatic in the manner of the above examples. This is simply illustrated by the case of my own company. If we publish textbooks for student librarians (as we do) and there are 10,000 student librarians in the world at any one time, we cannot sell more than 10,000 copies of any textbook; all the brilliant marketing ideas will not increase the number of potential customers. What marketing can do is to convert the actual sales achievement of, say, 30 per cent of the market into perhaps 40 per cent, or 50 per cent or more. But the ultimate market limit—which is not, of course, the numerical total of students, but only the greatest proportion of the total which could ever be persuaded into buying a textbook—cannot be increased by the publisher.

It follows that growth in conventional publishing is available only in two forms: (1) growth in scale by publishing more books or higher-price titles and achieving unchanged sales levels; (2) financial growth by (a) selling more copies of a constant number of titles without corresponding increases in running costs, or (b) increased profit margins (i.e. higher prices at reduced overheads) without corresponding loss of sales. Form (1) simply means the firm gets bigger in size of operation; form (2) means that it increases its profit return on capital employed. The first can be dramatic if the annual rate of output is suddenly doubled, or the firm takes over other lists and incorporates them in its own. The second can never be dramatic except fortuitously.

Expansion is dangerous, sharp expansion sharply dangerous. Whatever the method, expansion must be financed—the addition of extra titles involves production costs, extra sales involve extra selling expenditure, and increased margins the risk of reduced sales. This does not mean that expansion should not be undertaken. It *can't* not be undertaken. But it must be planned. Starting any business is 90 per cent special knowledge; running it is 90 per cent common sense— both include planning. Climbing mountains is also dangerous, but to some people desirable, so they achieve it by careful preparation, not by wandering up an unknown cliff on the spur of the moment.

Planned expansion is achieved by the preconsidered investment of resources—capacity in time, money and experience. In small businesses resources are scarce and the scale of investment in, say, one additional title, high in relation to the total of the firm's business.

The ratio of potential return to initial investment is nearly always constant, and it is therefore particularly important for the small publishing firm to seek steady growth rather than spectacular advance. The difficulties of producing three bestsellers in a short time within a small routine publishing programme can be frightful—in financing as well as in the administrative gearing necessary to service the bestsellers, which is immediately redundant when they swiftly die. It is worth remembering that a genuine expansion rate of 20 per cent a year (at the upper desirable level) only takes a 'micro-firm' from sales of £50,000 up to £60,000 the following year; but after ten years at that rate, the firm is selling more than £300,000 a year; and this scale of growth involves controllable stockbuilding, whereas dramatic growth cannot fail to incorporate heavy stockbuilding and liquidity risks.

Opportunities for the small firm

The analogy already used that a large publishing firm is in essence a collection of small firms hinges on the proposition that firms which are large are so because they publish more titles than small firms, not because they sell more copies of the average range of their products than would be sold if those products were published by different small firms. Clearly there are books where large resources of expenditure can achieve greater sales volume than would be available to a small firm, but if the average first printing in numbers of copies were calculated for all books published in the U.K., it is reasonable to expect that a considerable quantity of actual printing runs of books published by large firms would coincide with the industry's average. If it is the case that larger firms do not issue correspondingly larger editions, then it is only necessary to extrapolate the fact that all large firms cover a multiplicity of subject areas with different groups of publications in order to complete the analogy. Each subject group of standard-length editions corresponds with a separate small firm, and in operating its 'consortium of small firms', the large company achieves economy of scale in overhead costs by providing central services of production, administration, distribution, and so on. Only rarely will volume-of-title output influence printing costs over a programme. (Length of run, on the other hand, is the controlling factor in the unit cost of each single title.)

This being so, there ought to be no reason why large firms leave any gaps in any subject areas available for small firms to fill, since the published literature now embraces more or less every area of human endeavour and inquiry. There are, however, several reasons why gaps are continually available, the first arising from the extent of publishing's subject coverage. Knowledge is increasing so swiftly by volume, if not always in depth, that no single publishing entity can keep pace with its progress. In addition, as knowledge expands, the conceptualisation of knowledge fragments into more numerous and narrower subject compartments which, once defined, assume a generative impulse of their own towards expansion and subsequent refragmentation. Parkinson's law could be paraphrased as 'knowledge expands to fill the intellectual capacity available'.

Knowledge is not absolute, and communication is never objective. Therefore the opportunity for reinterpretation of knowledge is as infinite as the scope of the intellect. A single subject invariably permits more than a single book.

There is opportunity for the small firm to develop in subject specialisations so small that the profit potential is too low in money terms to attract large firms, even though correct profit percentages are obtainable. A publishing project yielding £1000 gross profit on manufacturing investment of the same amount might give a firm such as Longman–Penguins a net profit of 20 per cent on sales after allowing standard overhead percentage costs; but the actual money costs of drawing into operation a large-scale publishing mechanism for a small project might in practice destroy all the money profit.

Lastly, it is just as likely that a new field of publishing potential may first be discerned by a small publishing firm as by a large one.

Practical restrictions upon this theoretical equality of opportunity in obtaining materials for publication are mainly economic—the inability of the small firm to compete against large royalty advances, or guaranteed print runs which a team of representatives can place in the bookshops more certainly than those of a small firm. One consideration which may outweigh the restrictions is the ability of a small firm to devote more personal attention to the presentation of the book, or the advantageous marketing power which a specialist publisher has within his own subject field. The small publisher, almost by definition, specialises in one or more particular subject fields, usually excluding general books, though not always. The large publisher, as has been suggested, *covers* a range of subject fields, but probably without the intensity of concentration or the involvement of a small firm.

The small firm's search, therefore, is as much for new subject fields to expand into, as it is for individual new books within fields already published. They exist, but only as known fields hitherto underpublished in relation to apparent market capacity, or emergent fields of which the precise scope is blurred and only partly apparent to the prospecting publisher.

Advantages of small publishing operations

Let us consider the advantages in three groups: direct financial advantages, indirect financial advantages, non-financial advantages.

Axiomatically there are no *direct* financial advantages in a small operation as compared with a large one. This is to say that a firm does not make comparatively higher profit by reason of its size, except in one possible respect. There is a level of output up to which a small firm may be able to employ a lower ratio of staff to the numbers of titles published. Thus if a staff of four versatile and energetic people can efficiently operate a firm producing twenty new titles a year, it is almost certainly unlikely that a firm five times the size, with 100 new titles a year, can run on a staff of twenty. This is because in a small operation, many of the incidental tasks attached to a main function take up only minimal time for each separate book title, but when they cumulate over a large number of titles, they create staff demands of their own, staff creates additional administration, and so on. The result may be as shown in Table 1 on p. 56.

There can therefore be a contribution to profitability by savings on staff, accommodation and other 'human' costs. But the saving is cyclic in a growing small firm, for each stage of growth which increases staff neutralises the saving until full additional capacity is taken up. In addition, it is more difficult for a small firm to afford even a new executive secretary. On relative overheads of £20,000 and £80,000 for the small firm and the larger firm, a secretarial salary increases the former by $7\frac{1}{2}$ per cent and the latter by less than 2 per cent, requiring additional sales of revenue of 10 per cent and $2\frac{1}{2}$ per cent respectively to finance.

Indirect financial advantages, if regarded broadly as those which act towards stability or profitability without themselves being computable in money terms, are numerous.

Followers of special subject interests, educational or otherwise,

TABLE 1

20-title output		100-title output	
Job	Staff	Job	Staff
Overall management and administration	1	Administration: financial and office direction	1
Editorial and production work	1	bought ledger accounts	1
Sales and promotion	1	sales ledger accounts	1
Warehousing	1	stock and royalty records	1
Total	4	telephonist	1
		office junior/post	1 = 6
		Editorial:	
		editors	2
		secretarial	1 = 3
		Production:	
		production management	1
		production assistant	1
		secretarial	1 = 3
		Sales:	
		sales management	2
		sales assistant	1
		representation	4
		subsidiary rights	1
		invoice typing	4
		warehouse	4
		secretarial	2 = 18
			30

(Both totals of staffing are minimal and the large firm's membership of $7\frac{1}{2}$ times the small firm's for five times the new-title output does not mean the same ratios for the payrolls of each. The small firm employs at least three executives out of four employees, the large firm probably only five executives out of thirty total staff.)

have invariably been responsive to specialist publishing imprints actively intending to cater for their needs. The firm's executives can involve themselves in the area in which they are publishing, meeting authors and customers in person, obtaining direct 'feedback' from their personal contacts of books which are wanted, of sales angles which can be explored.

A small executive staff enables decisions to be taken quickly without formal consultation with other colleagues, and it reduces the friction between individuals, and time wasted in social contacts among them. There is no delay in exchanging information between departments, and no formal departmentalisation of functions which can mean that production work stops when the production manager falls ill.

There is also constant cross-fertilisation of ideas between executives—providing there is more than one. A publisher operating without executive staff, on the other hand, will actively miss the chance to discuss business and policy with anyone else.

A small firm is likely to publish its books more quickly after the acceptance of manuscripts. The several reasons for this include not only the executives' keenness to get books out into the market, but also the fact that the small publisher will not take on more titles than he can publish in a fixed period. The large firm is less inhibited by time considerations, and if it publishes in general fields it will be offered mostly finished manuscripts without much advance warning to plan them into a publishing programme. The publisher of commissioned books, as most small publishers are, whether they commission from an idea of their own or an author's outline project, can plan his programme months ahead of manuscript delivery. He must, however, make allowances in his programme for scripts which fail to arrive from their authors by the prescribed date.

Non-financial advantages (they might mostly be termed 'anti-financial') accrue to the publisher himself, and are often the main reason for a new publisher setting up his business. The independent small publisher is answerable to no one but himself in a way not open even to the titular head of a large organisation, for whom the benefit of outside shareholders and the need for political acquiescence by senior colleagues are commonly restrictive of his personal freedom within the business.

The implications of this argument, therefore, are several. There is considerable advantage in approaching any publishing project on a 'small' business level, rather than in terms of group activity. The development of special subject programmes can be made more easily viable if each is kept self-contained in administration, editorial selection and marketing opportunity, with the prospect of added savings when a group of self-contained programmes, or imprints, has emerged which can draw on basic group servicing facilities.

If, as is the case, the margins available for pricing books in relation to their manufacturing costs allow relatively little flexibility before market resistance occurs to publications which look manifestly over-priced in comparison with other books from other publishers, then it follows that the main area for increasing profitability lies in the publisher's other heads of cost—general overheads, distribution, trade terms and so on. The greatest opportunity for control of these lies with the self-contained 'small' imprint, which does not have to subscribe, for example, to the maximum trade discounts given on a publishing group's general book programme; or where it is not axio-matic that because the group has bought a computer, all group member's invoices must be processed through it, irrespective of the cost imputation to each member's individual profitability.

There are advantages in large-scale publishing, but the advantages lie almost entirely in the economics of scale produced by common services, and not in the expansion of the list to present a massive title output as one contained operation. For the same promotion manager (or sales manager) to handle an annual output of 300 titles with four assistants is the reverse of good sense. Those 300 titles cannot fail to encompass a number of quite distinct subject areas with very con-siderable variations in promotional and marketing requirements. What is needed is three (or four, or six) managers, each with his own defined area of marketing responsibility. The economy of scale comes, to take one example, when two or more of them pool into one envelope that portion of their mailing shots for which their address lists overlap.

So the role of the small publisher is really not a distinctive role at all. There is only the role of the publisher.

CHAPTER 3

METHOD—1. FINANCIAL

CHAPTER 2 described the general financial structure of the publishing operation. This chapter is concerned with the practical application of financial method to a (small) publishing house.

CAPITAL—NEEDS

Capital, the lump sum in hand at the outset of a business enterprise to be devoted to its furtherance, is in all cases the starting-point of that enterprise. It is axiomatic that money must first be spent before money can be made, and capital is the money used to promote a business so that earnings may be obtained from it. The first question to be asked, therefore, is how much capital is required to finance (i.e. promote) the enterprise which is contemplated.

Publishing is, as has been said earlier, a capital-intensive industry, and it is common to hear vast sums tossed into conversations about the amount of money needed to start a new firm. Estimates range from £5000 up to £100,000 and more. Generalisations such as this are, of course, irrelevant. The amount of capital required to start a new publishing business is the sum total of the following money requirements:

1. The cost of equipment and office premises which must be acquired—for the period from their acquisition until the business is trading sufficiently to meet any continuing part of them out of current earnings.
2. The cost of staff during the same period.

3. The cost of manufacturing or purchasing the product during the same period.

These three items, which break down into a large number of actual heads of expenditure, as we shall see in the next section on budgeting, represent exclusively the capital requirement, whether for a new enterprise or for the expansion of an existing one. It should be stressed that there is no point in having surplus capital idle on one side in anticipation of possible need later on. Money is expensive to have lying unused, and it must be assumed that the judgement which determines the total of the three items above is accurate. It is not hard to make it so, and misjudgement of financial needs at the outset of the enterprise is likely to be damaging and dangerous.

The actual amount which is calculated as necessary for the three items will vary according to the following criteria:

(a) the type of publication to be issued;
(b) the number of titles to be issued during an initial period;
(c) the extent to which the publisher can avoid normal business overhead costs by, for example, working from existing premises (his home), or can cut out employees by encompassing all the work himself;
(d) the extent of suppliers' credit available for the period between suppliers' invoice dates and the advent of trading income.

In a survey, in *The Author*, spring 1970, of recently established small publishers, Alex Hamilton found actual capital investment in several firms which began between 1966 and 1969 ranged from £6000 to £25,000. The firms in question, with one exception (£12,000 capital), publish general trade books, although within specific subject areas. All the figures given by Hamilton seem comparatively high in relation to the scale of the enterprises described and the consequent returns to be expected on the capital, particularly since all but one of the firms sub-contract (or did so) their sales representation and warehousing on a percentage-of-turnover basis, so that initial capital investment presumably excluded allocations for these costs. The sources of these capital sums were not given in the article.

My own starting capital consisted of £100 paid up as share capital, a bank overdraft of £500, plus extended credit of nine months from invoice date given by my printer (90 days from my binder) to a limit of £3000—of which some two-thirds was in fact utilised before we began to settle; say, working capital in one form or another of about £2500, and I found that the shortage of ready money concentrated the mind wonderfully. During my first ten months of trading, in 1965/6, this capital generated sales of £10,500.

CAPITAL—SOURCES

It is a harsh fact of life that capital from commercial sources of money is frequently only available to a business which can prove conclusively to the investor that it does not really require capital at all, at any rate, for the successful continuance of its present scale of operation. Publishing is regarded as a 'high-risk' industry, which hardly ever commends itself for investment at the embryo stage, and only rarely when the business is established with a regular profit record. Nevertheless, these sources of money should be mentioned, and possible investors fall into two groups: *commercial*—investment companies, merchant banks, clearing banks, existing publishing or other industrial companies; and *private*—personal finance, either one's own, one's family, or other private individuals.

Investment companies and merchant banks

There exists in all developed economies a number of investment companies and merchant banks which advertise regularly and prominently in the press their readiness to promote the development of private industry with loans. The advertisements should not be taken literally. These companies, which are accountable to their own shareholders for the conduct of their businesses, are not in the 'risk' industry, whatever their advertisements may say. They employ very carefully calculated formulae by which they judge the destinations of their funds, based especially on profit records and net assets, and even where the latter are available, the formulae applied are not designed to produce charitable contributions to the capital-seeker, but positive and substantial advantages for the investor. Thus, for example, any investment which is made in a small business will almost invariably require a participation in the equity capital, not so as to enable the investor to exercise any formal control (in the absence of crisis), but to obtain for him a share in the capital growth of the business (taxation is lower on capital appreciation than on current income).

It may be assumed for practical purposes that participation by this class of investor in a projected new publishing enterprise will not occur. For existing businesses which satisfy the preliminary requirements on profits and assets, the sort of proposition for investment most likely to be made is a loan for a specifically stated purpose, guaranteed personally by the borrower (not the borrowing company), carrying interest at current economic rates (1970: Bank Rate—7 per cent—plus another 8 per cent), either repayable within a term of years, or convertible on option into ordinary shares in the borrowing company at a stated future date, or else purchasing immediately a proportion of the equity of the company (usually 25–49 per cent— more than 25 per cent precludes the company from passing 'special resolutions', which require 75 per cent of the voting shares for approval, and represents some modest degree of control; for example, directors can only be removed from the board by special resolution).

It can be seen that, even when obtainable, money on these terms is expensive. The investment companies must themselves make profits for their shareholders, so that borrowers have, in one sense, to make a double set of profits out of money so borrowed—their own and the investor's; but the latter are invariably at pains to emphasise to a would-be borrower that he must be confident that the money they will lend him will be worth while to him in terms of the growth which it will achieve for the borrowing company.

Clearing banks

It is commonly held that overdraft finance from the clearing banks is the cheapest form of borrowed money. Interest rates are geared in some form to Bank Rate, which is effectively the lowest common denominator of prevailing commercial interest rates. Clearing banks are commercial organisations too, of course, but with vast sums of liquid cash from depositors available to them, they are able to spread their investments more thinly and more widely than can any single investment company and, by their size, to participate more fully in the transitory manifestations of government policy (e.g. priority for export finance). They are not, however, 'investors' in the institutional sense, but a source of short-term finance provided against the deposit (rather than the purchase) of security.

My own experience with my bank has been entirely satisfactory. Its managers are shrewd and not given to risk-taking, but a detailed project with satisfactory forecast evidence of its potential stability, and accompanied by personal guarantees from the borrower of any loan (the deposit of securities such as life-insurance policies, title deeds, share or unit trust certificates), should be sufficient to secure an overdraft contribution to the capital required. In my own case, the securities I was able to deposit did not cover in value the amount I sought to borrow, but the bank manager declared himself ready to bridge the modest gap on the evidence provided by the conduct of my personal bank account during the preceding seven years and because, he said, the two or three life-insurance policies which I then had in force satisfied him that I was, by nature, a 'saver'! He took some risk in granting me the overdraft, but in all the circumstances it was not large—though it must be admitted that his successor a couple of years later revealed to me, when agreeing to increase our overdraft facility, that he personally would not have taken the initial risk which his predecessor had taken! Obviously, at some stage in the search for capital, a degree of luck enters, though it may be argued that the later manager was talking retrospectively and therefore academically, not as one faced with the immediate circumstances of his predecessor.

The clearing bank, therefore, should be the first organisation to approach, and its reaction to an overdraft request for a particular business project can be regarded as some external evidence of the project's viability. The proviso is that the bank will make only a small contribution in money terms. It may be high as a proportion of the total capital requirements, but it will not run into many hundreds of pounds unless the security is first of all there to guarantee it.

Publishing or other industrial companies

Although the growth of 'conglomerates'—holding companies with a diversity of industrial interests and operations under their ownership or control—has caught up a number of publishing companies, especially in the U.S.A., this outside participation is not likely to be available to a new enterprise. The theory behind the conglomerate is not just diversification for its own sake, but also in order to develop a stable of established companies which can to some extent intertrade, while drawing on central services for structural and financial administration. Thus, for example, a paper group may buy into publishing in part to channel some of its paper products to the publishing company —less for the additional business to be obtained, unless the publishing company is very large, than to divert to it periodic excess capacity or surplus production; and also in many cases to be able to integrate the managements of broadly similar operations, with consequent economies of scale.

But although a new publisher is unlikely to obtain backing from other areas of industry, it does sometimes happen that an existing publishing company is prepared to support in some way a nominally independent imprint. The independence may be restricted to editorial decisions, or may extend to the whole operation. One of Britain's few women publishers began an imprint of her own a few years ago with complete editorial freedom, while retaining her existing and separate job with a large company, which additionally provided her with sales and distribution services. Another new publisher linked up with a printing and publishing company in a joint and independent imprint, in which the finance was provided by the printer, who also undertook most of the new firm's production work. The formal term for an arrangement like this is 'joint venture'.

Clearly, it is possible for a would-be independent with a seemingly sound editorial project, no source of capital, but a reluctance to exploit the idea from the status of a mere employee, to reach agreement with an established firm which will give some measure of independence. But an arrangement of this kind must, at best, take second place to true independence, not only for the limitations of freedom which it imposes in practice, but also because of the pressure which the fostering company must increasingly exert, if the 'independent' is successful, for its full integration with the parent operation. A breakout by an independent from this position, in the event of success, is only possible if the original agreement has been drawn on terms which are unlikely to have been available to the independent unless the parent company had approached the arrangement with either uneconomic benevolence or carelessness. In the event of failure, a breakout may be worth while if the failure is due solely to pressures exerted by the parent, but not otherwise. Correspondingly, the pressure for severance may come more strongly from the foster-parent if its publishing offspring fails to produce the results forecast or, by some quirk of trade, ceases to fit logically into the parent's operation.

Trade credit

This is an extremely important and often under-rated source of capital; though that does not mean that it is necessarily easier to obtain than more orthodox money. In terms of capital, trade credit from suppliers means from printers and/or binders, since it is the manufacturing costs of the product which constitute by far the largest amount of expenditure for a new or small company.

Printers (or binders) willing to offer extended credit of six to twelve months from invoice date for a completed job (as against the norm of sixty to ninety days) may be motivated in several different ways. They may have surplus capacity; they may share the publisher's enthusiasm for his project as a good potential growth field; they may be impressed simply by the business qualities which they discern in the publisher, or they may be chronically short of work (as distinct from having some spare capacity). Often the motive may be a mixture of these, but the publisher is well advised to beware of the last category, for the printer who is chronically short of work may be so for a good reason—over-pricing, inferior quality, inability to maintain completion dates—and if the printer folds, so does the publisher's operational base.

A publisher soliciting trade credit must keep in mind the fact that

a printer who grants it has taken a straightforward business decision
—to wait for his money in return for an assurance of profitable work—
which does not thereafter place the publisher in an inferior position,
unable to demand the expected standards of performance, whether of
quality, efficiency or attention. In addition, it should be remembered
that the credit will be charged for, probably not by so crude a yardstick as formal interest, but by higher estimates for each job than are
made to a customer paying cash at thirty days.

If the idea behind the publishing project is sound, then print credit
is pretty sure to be obtainable somewhere. This means that books can
be finished and sold and some earnings from them received before
their manufacturing costs become payable. But the publisher must
always be selective, paradoxical though this may sound, about the
firms from which he solicits extended credit. It is probably true to
say that very few of the imprints founded in the twentieth century
have not had to some degree the advantage of print credit beyond the
normal trade average.

But although print credit represents a substantial contribution to
capital needs, it does not meet them in full.

Self credit

Under the general heading of *private*, as distinct from *commercial*
investment, the publisher's own resources come first into consideration. In an economic and social environment turned towards the
conversion of private capital into public income (by reason of the
taxation which income attracts and static capital does not) there are
now comparatively few people with resources which can be turned
into significant amounts of money, or on which money can be realised.
House mortgage is the most obvious device, or second mortgage,
subject to the proviso that second mortgages are usually available only
for short terms and at monstrous rates of interest which it may not be
possible for a new commercial enterprise to cover. If a second mortgage is the only source of capital and costs, for example, 20 per cent
in interest, the capital investment in a publishing enterprise must
yield from the outset more than 20 per cent, potential capital gain
included, or this source of finance is uneconomic. Re-mortgaging,

however, may be possible—the cancellation of an existing partly-paid mortgage, and its replacement by a new one, to provide a capital surplus—at normal market rates of interest.

Family or friends

There is little to say under this head. Either a publisher has family or friends sufficiently attracted by the glamour of association with publishing or confident of the publisher's abilities to lay money on the line—or he has not.

If he has, it is worth remarking that the use of family money can often bring its own embarrassments, not confined to a parade of the *magna opera* written by members of the family in years gone by and ever after confined to dark cupboards until the rise of 'a publisher in the family'; also, wealthy aunts benevolent at the outset of a publishing enterprise may often cease to be so at the end of the fifth year of successive balance-sheet losses.

Private individuals

The columns of the 'quality' and financial press commonly contain advertisements from private individuals with capital at their disposal, seeking to invest in 'sound' business projects. There are two points to be made about this source of finance.

First of all, a new enterprise can hardly be identified as 'sound' until it has been entered upon.

Secondly, these private investors are, without exception, seeking to buy the 'know-how' of someone with an idea but no money. If all they required was 'sound' investment, the opportunities in established commercial operations are unlimited. But these people are invariably without serviceable occupations themselves and wish to back a viable business idea on terms which, in a crunch, would leave them on top; and any crunch with their investees would not be precipitated until the investor had learned all that the publisher had to teach him about the chosen field.

Of all potential investors, the private stranger is perhaps the least disinterested in the actual nature of the project mooted, and thus the one to be regarded with the greatest suspicion.

This brief description of the possible sources of capital has concentrated on new projects, for the simple reason that existing publishing operations either require finance for new developments, in which case they may be regarded as 'new' projects, with the added advantage of previous operations by which their proposals may to some extent be judged—or else they require it to subsidise the continuance of an already sinking operation, in which case finance will be difficult to obtain. It does not, and is not intended to, reveal a situation weighted in favour of the borrower, for it is not so weighted in reality, and there exists no formal system in the British economy for the dispassionate financial support of future endeavour on a comparatively small scale.

The point, therefore, is that it is desirable to keep capital requirements for a business enterprise to the lowest level possible without damaging the projected shape of the enterprise, and this is not simply to avoid watering down the entrepreneur's interest by incorporating the backing of others, but also because, as has been said, a shortage of money at the outset wonderfully concentrates the mind.

The optimum procedure for obtaining capital—and I speak from my personal experience and circumstances, which may be variable in the case of another—is a combination of the publisher's own resources, plus trade credit, plus bank overdraft, in a total calculated by the most careful forward budgeting; to which subject we now turn.

BUDGETING

This vital part of the business function is discussed under three headings: A. *Expenditure budgeting*, which breaks down into two sub-categories—capital budgeting (the preliminary estimates of set-up costs), and operational budgeting (covering running overheads and manufacture)—B. *Sales forecasting*, and C. *Cash-flow budgeting* (the balance of actual income against actual expenditure, as distinct from the calculation of profit and loss.

A. *Expenditure budgeting*

1. CAPITAL BUDGETING. I am here concerned with budgeting for actual starting expenditure, so by 'capital' in this context I mean a total available sum of ready cash, not necessarily to be devoted only

to items which may be legitimately charged to 'capital', as against current trading, in a balance sheet.

Capital being required, as we have seen, to meet all expenditure incurred between the time of commencing the enterprise and the point at which trading revenue begins to equal operating expenditure on a regular and sustainable basis, the uses of this capital may be examined in three time-phases—initial and outright equipment purchase; starting costs up to the point at which trading begins; and the 'shortfall' period between commencement of trading and the equalisation of revenue and expenditure. The order of listing is roughly the order in which costs are likely to be incurred over a period of time.

(a) *Outright purchase* may cover some of the following items: (i) Premises—if a lump sum is paid as purchase price or premium for offices and/or warehouse, including necessary decoration or fit-out costs (e.g. telephone installation, heaters). (ii) Administration—legal fees for forming a company or drawing up a partnership deed, and for conveyancing of premises. Artist's fees for designing stationery, publisher's device, house style. (iii) Office equipment—desks, chairs, filing cabinets, typewriters, adding machine, mechanical accounting system or account books, photocopier, nameplate, initial stocks of printed stationery (letterheads, invoice forms, statements, etc.) and small stationery. (iv) Publicity—normally a new firm will not spend money on advertising until it has a product to sell, but there may be, for example, a single-shot paid announcement in the press. (v) Transport—purchase of car or delivery van.

(b) *Starting costs* from inception up to the trading point, a period which must be known or estimated accurately in advance. (i) Premises —rent, rates, heat, light, telephone, office cleaning, repairs or replacements, insurances. (ii) Administration—publisher's remuneration, staff wages and salaries, state welfare contributions, office tea and coffee, etc., legal and professional fees, bank charges. (iii) Office materials—stationery, postage and carriage, trade periodicals, packing materials. (iv) Publicity—media advertising, pamphlets, catalogues, brochures, entertainment. (v) Transport—travel costs, including cost of running office vehicles. (vi) Manufacture (costs not likely to be incurred on extended credit)—royalty advances to authors, design fees, blockmaking costs, copyright fees, jacket lamination.

(c) *The shortfall period* involves the same heads of expenditure as the starting period up to trading, but we must assume that it terminates (when revenue equals or exceeds expenditure) before the extended credit invoices for printing and binding begin to fall due, so these main manufacturing costs are excluded. The starting costs are, however, augmented now by increased levels in some heads of expenditure as a result of the commencement of trading—warehousing staff, postage and carriage on books sold, stationery and packing materials, transport costs, insurances.

However, the duration of the shortfall period can only be determined by making at this stage the first sales and revenue forecast. The entire enterprise will have been founded upon a general expectation of demand for the proposed product, leading progressively to more exact estimates of the sales potential of the individual titles planned to comprise the starting list. What must now be formulated is not only a precise estimate of sales, title by title, and revenue to be derived from them, but also a time schedule, first for the period over which the sales revenue will be achieved by invoice, and secondly for the additional length of time before customers settle the invoices.

It is obviously difficult to lay down any general rules for sales forecasting over a new list; the firm's imprint and its publications are untested, there may or may not be a co-edition with an American publisher, or sheet sales elsewhere overseas. But the publisher will have done some market research before embarking on his project—at a later stage, before the appearance of his first titles, he will have visited bookshops, libraries and other potential customers, to obtain a more precise idea of initial sales—and he must now formulate, as cautiously as possible, some basis for estimating pre-publication orders, and the immediate flow of orders just after publication, when a title has been listed in the *British National Bibliography*, and the general nature of sales to be expected thereafter—for example, steady for a period, seasonal in time with academic syllabuses, or swiftly declining to a trickle.

As far as customers' credit is concerned, this too varies, but in the absence of special inducements (e.g. extra discounts) for quick settlement, it is reasonable to assume that customers overseas will take three to six months from invoice date to settle. The U.K. customers' payments can be expected to follow a pattern something like this: in first month after invoice date, 15–20 per cent of the previous month's turnover; in the second month after invoice date, 40 per cent; in the third month, 30 per cent; later than this, 10–15 per cent. This presupposes an average U.K. credit period of about three months. If, therefore, turnover is planned to increase each month over the previous month, it is fairly safe to say that from the fourth month after the commencement of trading, the average monthly receipts should not be less than the total (U.K.) turnover in the first month. But growth thereafter will not, of course, be *pro rata* from month to month. When under full operation, revenue budgeting is best done on three-month averages, taking into account seasonal fluctuations (most booksellers, for example, are too busy *selling* books in December to have time to pay for them), and differential credit periods taken by overseas customers, in which a main factor is market distance from the U.K. and the consequent transportation time for goods to it.

We are now ready to relate these different heads of budgeted expenditure together, and by incorporating the sales forecast just described to reach a total of starting cash requirements (printing and binding costs excluded). If capital is deliberately allowed to meet the production costs of early titles, with or without extended credit facilities also, the known totals can be added to the (basically overhead) total in Fig. 1.

2. OPERATIONAL BUDGETING. For the regular budgeting necessary to control an existing operation, the task is broadly the same as was outlined under 'capital budgeting', except that in that case we were concerned with determining a specific sum of money which would be required for starting a new operation, whereas the purpose of operational budgeting is to establish the profit to be derived from the operation already in force, and in doing so to provide a series of yardsticks for expenditure under different headings, against which outturn (what actually happens) can be measured, as a control of the overall enterprise.

Budgeting for actual operation, therefore, will be on a balance-

Fig. 1. Capital Budgeting by Time of Expenditure for a New Enterprise

Head of expenditure	(a) Outright purchase	(b) Starting costs for an estimated six-month period between inception and the commencement of trading	(c) The shortfall for an estimated period averaging three months
(i) Premises	purchase or premium* redecoration/alteration* fit out costs: telephone heating lighting	rent rates heat and light telephone cleaning repairs insurances:† premises contents	rent rates heat and light telephone cleaning repairs insurances:† premises contents
(ii) Administration	legal fees: company formation conveyance design fee	publisher's remuneration staff wages and salaries state welfare contributions office sundries legal fees audit fees bank charges insurances:† employer's liability third party	publisher's remuneration staff wages and salaries: office staff warehouse staff state welfare contributions: office staff warehouse staff legal fees audit fees bank charges insurances:† employer's liability third party stock goods in transit credit

(iii) Office materials	furniture:* desks chairs carpets filing cabinets shelves and cupboards equipment:* typewriters adding machine accounting system photocopier stationery nameplate	stationery† trade periodicals postage and carriage	stationery: letterheads, etc. invoices and statements packing materials
(iv) Publicity	media advertising(?)	media advertising pamphlets brochures catalogues entertainment	media advertising pamphlets brochures catalogues entertainment
(v) Transport	purchase of car or van*	vehicle running costs other travel	vehicle running costs: office use dispatch use
(vi) Manufacture	—	royalty advances† design fees blockmaking costs copyright fees jacket lamination	royalty advances† design fees blockmaking costs copyright fees jacket lamination
	Total Costs	Total Costs	Total Costs

add (b)   Total Costs
add (c)   Total Costs
=   Total Costs

Grand Total of capital sum required, assuming that the monthly total of sales revenue after three months' trading will be equal to or in excess of the monthly running costs.

N.B.: 1. Items marked * are chargeable in the annual balance sheet as capital expenditure and allowable for depreciation.
    2. All other items represent trading costs which are chargeable against profit for taxation purposes, except that items marked † may not be chargeable in full in the year they are incurred (i.e. may be carried forward, either complete, or in part, or after writing down in value).
    3. Entertainment, (iv) (b), is not allowable against profits for tax purposes, except entertainment of foreign potential customers.

sheet basis, not cash flow, but it still consists of listing all the likely heads of expenditure during a future period, with qualified forecasts of the sum of each. The division to be used will be into running costs (overheads), and manufacturing costs.

Running costs. The debit side of a publisher's annual trading account reveals clearly how expenditure falls into two categories: the cost of physical manufacture of the product to be sold, and the cost of running the business operation which manufactures and sells that product (see specimen balance sheet, Fig. 7, on pp. 84–85).

Running costs, therefore, are those heads of expenditure which are not contributions to the physical manufacture of the books, and they include some or all of those listed in Fig. 2.

FIG. 2. RUNNING COSTS

Rent and rates ⎫
Heat and light   ⎪
Telephone   ⎬   (*cost of premises*)
Repairs   ⎪
Cleaning   ⎭
Wages, salaries and welfare contributions (*cost of staff*)
Packing materials
Postage and dispatch costs
Insurances
Stationery
Advertising and publicity
Travelling and entertainment
Bad debts
Professional fees
Representation

There may be other heads, but in each operation there will already have been listed under capital budgeting (Fig. 1) a very full list. For operational budgeting this list must be redrawn and forecast in money terms for an annual (or shorter) period of operation.

This involves more variables than the capital budgeting already described, because of the difficulty of forecasting sales over as long a period as one year. Higher sales than expected will require more expenditure on dispatch and warehousing costs, and perhaps on staff. However, if the enterprise is in operation, either newly so or well established, then past trading gives a yardstick for estimating, even if it is only the successful completion of the third capital budgeting phase—the period from commencement of trading to equalisation of cash flow. Thus some evidence for sales expectations is available (if the capital budgeting phase has *not* been successfully completed, then the enterprise is presumably not in operation anyway), and the important point to remember is that the higher than expected sales of already available products will, subject to correct margins, generate their own additional revenue to meet higher running costs, at least after the customer-credit period has elapsed.

The budgeting, can, therefore, be done on the basis provided by the capital budget, and the total anticipated expenditure under its different heads can be costed.

Manufacturing costs. Expenditure on manufacture may, for each title, involve some or all of the items shown in Fig. 3 on p. 76.

Any fees payable other than listed in Fig. 3 should be included (e.g. readers' advisory fees), unless they are chargeable to the author, in which case they represent a diminution of author's earnings, instead of a manufacturing cost.

As accurate an estimate as possible must be made and totalled up from these heads for each title to be published in the twelve-month period under budget, but not including work in progress on books to be published in the subsequent period, since this is carried forward into the accounts for that period.

Thus we now have forecasts of all anticipated manufacturing and running costs for the year ahead. We now turn to the other side of the coin—revenue.

B. *Sales forecasting*

The initial problem here may be different from that for an established operation, if the enterprise is newly formed. The forecast of

FIG. 3. MANUFACTURING COSTS

Graphic design: dustjacket
                   book typography and layout
                   illustrations artwork (or print purchase costs)

Blockmaking: dustjackets
                   illustrations and/or embellishments

Printing: composition:
                       hot metal *or*
                       cold type *or*
                       photo offset from U.S. edition (fee payable to U.S.
                           publisher), or from another publisher's earlier
                           edition
                   imposition (make up of pages)
                   machining

Paper: text paper
                   illustrations paper
                   dustjacket paper
                   printed endpapers

Binding: casebinding
                   folding
                   collating
                   sewing
                   casing-in
                   jacketing
                   spine brasses

---

sales revenue derives in the first instance from the selling prices of the products, and whereas the existing business already has a pricing policy, the new one has yet to calculate a formula for pricing its products.

All sales forecasting starts, paradoxically enough, with the forecasts of expenditure—the revenue needed from sales to meet total costs and provide a desired profit. But the sales forecast—or, more exactly, the overall budget for the whole operation—reveals to the existing publisher how many units he has to sell, from established margins, before he makes a profit, yet to the new publisher what margins he must fix, in order to make a profit, from presupposed unit sales.

At the start of his sales forecasting, therefore, the existing publisher will work as follows:

(i) Estimate sales for the year of back list titles, and calculate the revenue to accrue from them, less the value of the books sold in his balance sheet at the end of the previous accounting period, and the author's royalties payable on them.

(ii) Multiply his total manufacturing cost of new titles to be published by whatever factor the firm uses for pricing its products to give gross published price revenue; then reduce this by trade discount and author's royalty percentages to show gross turnover expectation from sales of all copies of all new titles.

(iii) Deduct the figure calculated in (i) above from the expenditure budget total, to leave a balance to be met from new title sales.

(iv) The balance arrived at in (iii) is then expressed as a percentage of the figure achieved in (ii), as a guide to the *average* proportion of the edition of each new title which must be sold before a profit over and above residual stock values starts to be made.

This procedure gives the existing publisher a yardstick of *necessary* unit sales. A title-by-title, re-estimate of likely sales, based on his own judgement, gives a different estimate for total potential sales revenue. If the *necessary* sales figure is unduly high, and *likely* sales fall short of the expenditure budget, then margins (or the editorial policy) need revision. Otherwise, the *necessary* sale provides a working control for current operations during the period under review, and the greater the upward difference between it and the *likely* sale, taken as a target, the greater the potential profit.

The new publisher, on the other hand, has only his own title-by-title assessments of likely unit sales on which to base his sales revenue forecasts. If they are significantly too high his operation collapses. It must therefore be assumed that they are substantially correct, and the unit sales forecasts then used as a basis for pricing and margin-fixing.

Pricing involves the matching of all the shares in the ultimate consumer's purchase payment to the amount of that payment. The payment is shared four ways: by manufacturer(s), wholesalers/retailers, author and publisher. Only one of these shares is a fixed sum, expressible in money irrespective of the book's selling price, and that is the manufacturer's share, calculated as a 'unit cost' in pounds or pence for each saleable copy manufactured. The author and the seller receive their shares as a prearranged percentage of the selling price, the remainder of which, after settling the manufacturer, goes to the publisher. In fixing a published price, therefore, the publisher must be able to convert his total annual running cost into an accurate percentage of his total sales revenue, and then apply the same calculation to a single book in order to arrive at the published price.

So a new publisher begins with his twin forecasts of expenditure and revenue, the former calculated as on page 72, the latter grossed up from his presupposed unit sales of new publications. If he is wise he adds a margin of error of, say, 10 per cent to budget costs, and deducts the same percentage from forecast revenue. He can thus express the former as a percentage of the latter and, by tying it in with the percentage share-out of consumer payment for one book, first achieve an economic published price for that book, and then extrapolate a general policy for pricing.

It works out as shown in Fig. 4, on a per-copy basis.

There are two points to be made now. First of all the profit is shown as 10 out of 100, but 100 is what the ultimate consumer pays to the seller; it is not what the publisher receives as his sales revenue, which is the published price less the seller's discount, i.e. $100 - 35 = 65$. A profit of 10 on revenue of 65 is approximately 15 per cent.

Secondly, the manufacturer's share is, as we have seen, the only sum fixed in advance, and after all the other shares have been worked out it can be seen to be, at 20, just 5 times the eventual published price. So a *general* rule of pricing can be derived from this as

FIG. 4. PUBLISHED PRICE BREAKDOWN

Manufacturing cost	20
Author royalty	10
Publisher overhead	25 (approximately 40 per cent of sales revenue)
Seller's discount (average)	35
	90
Profit	10
	100 = selling price

---

follows: provided the author's royalty remains at 10 per cent of the published price, the seller's discount at 35 per cent of the published price and the publisher's running costs at 40 per cent of his sales revenue (or 25 per cent of the published price), then the published price of any book can be set at 5 times the unit manufacturing cost in order to show a profit for the publisher of 15 per cent on his sales revenue—less the depreciation incurred on unsold stock by writing down the value below cost. In other words, the profit is only as high as 15 per cent if either all copies of the edition are sold, or unsold copies continue to be valued at cost.

For any new publisher, these indications of pricing and forecasting must provide only a general set of rules, which he must watch most carefully from title to title, and be prepared to vary as practical necessity may declare in any set of circumstances. Budgeting and forecasting are inevitably imprecise, but provided the new publisher is cautious in his expectations of revenue and generous in his forecast of expenditure, a surplus of the former over the latter should ensue for long enough to establish a case history of actual results and experience on which far more accurate financial prognostication can be based. One of the most startlingly successful new British publishers of the 1960s told me how for several years his forecasts of revenue were always exceeded and his estimates of expenditure too large—to such profit that he was eventually able to appoint a qualified financial director in his company. Shortly after this, both sets of monthly forecasts began regularly to coincide most closely with the eventual out-turn, and when the publisher complained about the disappearance of the monthly trading 'bonuses' to which he had grown accustomed, the financial director replied 'But of course—you employed me to make *accurate* forecasts, not to deliver problematical bonuses!'.

We now turn to a matter of high relevance to the publishing industry—the difference between balance-sheet results and cash flow (in budgeting terms), before consolidating this section by a general examination of the balance sheet, the yardstick of financial performance in a capitalist society.

C. *Cash-flow budgeting*

In the accounts, the results declared on the profit and loss account show whether a firm has made a profit or a loss in a given period of trading. Cash-flow budgeting and analysis, on the other hand, reveals whether a publishing enterprise has enough money in the bank at the end of each month to pay the bills which must be paid.

We start, obviously, with the expenditure budget, calculated (p. 72) on an annual basis. Not only does cash-flow budgeting have to subdivide the expenditure budget into monthly proportions; it must also make cash provision for those items of expenditure in the annual budget which are paid on a non-monthly basis. Thus the heads of expenditure shown in Figs. 2 and 3 for running costs and manufacturing costs have to be subdivided again, this time on a time basis, as in Fig. 5, and after calculating what is considered to be the length of credit allowable both to customers and from suppliers.

When all possible heads of expenditure have been listed and estimated—allowances are made on a monthly basis for random heads, such as repairs, which may or may not occur without notice—the items can then be rearranged on a calendar basis. But it must be remembered that the periodic heads—all those payable quarterly or less frequently—do not necessarily coincide with the quarter day of the year, so adjustment must be made for variations. Thus, if the telephone is installed, for example, in April, the first rental demand

Fig. 5. Time Analysis of Payments

All heads of expenditure	Monthly		3 monthly		6 monthly		Annual	Extraordinary	Total
		or		or		or			
Rent			X						4X
Rates					X				2X
Heat and light			X						4X
Telephone			X						4X
Repairs	X								12X
Cleaning	X								12X
Wages and salaries	X								12X
Welfare contributions	X								12X
Packing materials			X						4X
Stationery: printed			X						4X
general	X								12X
Advertising and publicity	X								12X
Travel	X								12X
Entertainment	X								12X
Postage and carriage	X								12X
Trade periodicals	X								12X
Insurances							X		X
Sundries	X								12X
Bank charges			X						4X
Loan interest	X		X		X		X		X
Accountancy fees							X		X
Legal fees							X		X
Taxation								X	?

FIG. 6. BUDGETING FOR TIME OF PAYMENTS

January	monthly	
February	,,	
March	,,	+ 3 monthly
April	,,	
May	,,	
June	,,	+ 3 monthly + 6 monthly
July	,,	
August	,,	
September	,,	+ 3 monthly
October	,,	
November	,,	
December	,,	+ 3 monthly + 6 monthly + annually

Plus extraordinary payments (taxation, etc.) budgeted for as and when the accountant advises they will become due. Taxation will be discussed later in this chapter as part of 'Profit measurement'.

may come in May, and thereafter in August, November and February. The next list must lay out these infrequent payments when they occur, and the strict obedience here to the calendar year is merely exemplary (see Fig. 6).

These two very simple time charts should reveal quite clearly that cash-flow budgeting is little more than common-sense scheduling of the various payments enumerated in the more formal expenditure budget. Manufacturing costs are not included in them, because these must be scheduled separately, title by title, according to the credit terms negotiated with printer and binder. After a starting period for the initial credit, therefore, each month is likely to see a manufacturing payment added to the running costs itemised above. In addition, every six months the accumulated author's royalties have to be settled, usually according to the calendar year, in September and March, and they must be allowed for, on an estimate based on the sales forecast. One further point about manufacturing costs is that many of the smaller items will not admit of extended credit or be worth it—for example, jacket design and blockmaking costs—and these must be allowed for settlement in the monthly budget, but on a 'job' basis, rather than by a general allocation in each month's budget to cover approximate amounts.

Cash-flow budgeting is thus comparatively simple for running costs, but in order to meet manufacturing costs a close examination of the publishing programme, title by title, is required to ensure that the incidentals of this area of expenditure—including such things as reprints and rebinds—are allowed for.

The maxim most worth remembering in budgeting for cash flow, which is the real test of financial administration in publishing, is 'never cheat yourself'. In balance-sheet budgeting for profit, some flexibility is available according to market circumstances in valuing stock in hand. But in cash flow, you can only kid yourself, and over-optimism is a sure path to the law-courts.

Lastly, in this very long subsection, let us look at and comment on an active balance-sheet, before we move from there to a consideration of profit measurement.

It can be seen from the sample accounts outlined on pp. 84–85 (Fig. 7) that annual accounts consist of two main parts, namely the Profit and Loss Account and the Balance Sheet.

The Profit and Loss Account is a summary of the trading results for a given period (usually a year but can be either longer or shorter) and normally coincides with the state of the Balance Sheet. Consequently it only deals with items of a revenue nature, i.e. sales, costs of sale, overhead expenses and exceptional items such as taxation, legal and litigation costs and the like.

The Balance Sheet is a statement at any given date of the assets and liabilities of a firm. Herein the effects of all previous results are accumulated and the net worth of the business, i.e. the excess of assets over liabilities, calculated.

Comparison is, of course, the key to reading a balance sheet, and the following list gives some of the main points to be looked for (by an investor) and provided for (by the management of the business).

Fig. 7

SNIPCOCK AND TWEED (BOOK PUBLISHERS) LTD.

Trading & Profit & Loss Account

For year ended 31st December 1970

Trading Account

1969 £		1970 £	1970 £		1969 £	1970 £
34,680	Stock in hand and work in progress as at 1st January 1970	33,290		Sales	104,710	136,910
47,730	Purchases, production and manufacturing costs	68,640				
82,410			101,930			
33,290	Less closing stock and work in progress as at 31st December 1970		40,260			
49,120			61,670			
15,520	Authors royalties and fees		18,490			
64,640			80,160			
40,070	Gross profit—carried down		56,750			
£104,710			£136,910		£104,710	£136,910

Profit & Loss Account

1969 £		1970 £	1970 £		1969 £	1970 £
16,710	Wages, salaries and commissions (incl. state welfare)	25,360		Gross profit—brought down	40,070	56,750
380	Travel and entertainment	720				
2300	Rent and rates	2300				
540	Heating and lighting	620				
290	Telephone	280				
70	Repairs	100				
120	Cleaning	140				
400	Insurances	440				
2400	Packing materials and stationery	2810				
1680	Advertising and publicity	1840				
3500	Postage and despatch costs	4680				
260	Bank interest and charges	280				
420	Accounting fees	500				
220	Legal fees	100				
800	Provision for bad debts	1640				
400	Depreciation	500				
200	Sundry trade expenses	240				
30,470			42,550			
9600	Balance—carried down		14,200			
£40,070			£56,750		£40,070	£56,750

PROFIT & LOSS ACCOUNT (cont.)

1969 £		1970 £	1970 £		1969 £	1970 £
8000	Directors' remuneration	12,000		Balance—brought down	9600	14,200
720	Provision for taxation	935		Balance brought forward from previous years	4555	5435
5435	Balance carried forward		6700			
£14,155			£19,635		£14,155	£19,635

Fig. 7

SNIPCOCK AND TWEED (BOOK PUBLISHERS) LTD.

Balance-Sheet

As at 31st December 1970

Capital and Liabilities

	1969 £		1970 £		
CAPITAL					
AUTHORISED					
20,000 ordinary shares of £1 each	20,000			20,000	
ISSUED AND FULLY PAID					
13,000 ordinary shares of £1 each	13,000			13,000	
REVENUE RESERVES					
Profit and loss account—					
Balance of undistributed profits	5435			6700	
	18,435			19,700	
PROVISION FOR TAXATION	1465			2400	
PROVISION FOR DELAPIDATION	900			900	
CURRENT LIABILITIES					
Bank overdraft	1880			900	
Sundry trade creditors	23,180		32,420		
Sundry liabilities	8810		11,380		
	33,870			46,470	
	£54,670			£69,470	

Assets

	1969 £			1970 £		
FIXED ASSETS						
Leasehold property (at cost)	3000			3000		
Less accumulated depreciation	2990			2990		
		10			10	
Office and warehouse equipment (at cost)	3200			3200		
Less accumulated depreciation	1400			1800		
		1800			1400	
Motor vehicles (at cost)	1680			1680		
Less accumulated depreciation	820			920		
		860			760	
			2670			2170
CURRENT ASSETS						
Stock and work in progress		33,290			40,260	
Sundry debtors		16,200			22,200	
Prepaid expenses		2200			4800	
Cash in hand and at bank		310			40	
			52,000			67,300
			£54,670			£69,470

SIGNED:

_____ Director

_____ Secretary

Report of the Auditors to the members of Snipcock and Tweed (Book Publishers) Ltd.

In our opinion the balance sheet and profit and loss account of Snipcock and Tweed (Book Publishers) Limited together with the notes relating thereto, comply with the requirements of the Company Acts 1948 and 1967, and give respectively a true and fair view of the company's affairs as at 31st December 1970 and its profit for the year ended on that date.

Bloodhound House,
London E.C.2.
2nd June 1971

Tickit & Run
Chartered Accountants

THE BALANCE SHEET

Capital

1. The statement of capital authorised is a piece of technical information. The capital issued and paid up, however, is important since this is a liability on the part of the company to its shareholders which continues throughout corporate life. The sum shown is the initial amount provided to finance the operation, with any later additions. It does not include reinvestment of trading income in further purchases of goods or services.

Revenue reserves

2. This includes the balance on the profit and loss account which shows the accumulated surpluses or deficits after tax which the company has recorded since it began its trading life, together with any transfers to general reserve, and remains a charge upon the company which is attributable to its members.

3. The remaining items on the left-hand (liabilities) side of the page are the various moneys owed by the company, with taxation incurred on past profits, but not yet due for payment, and depreciations expected to the company's assets, shown separately. The 'Sundry liabilities' item may, if desired, be analysed more fully to show the firm's non-trade debts (royalties, rents, etc.).

4. The right-hand (assets) side of the page shows the value which the company owns to set against its liabilities. They are self-explanatory, with some qualifications. For example, the figure shown for repayments covers such items as advances paid to authors before publication of their books, and pre-publication manufacturing costs, such as illustration and blockmaking costs, design and copyright fees, as well as overheads such as rent, insurances, rates, motor vehicle tax and insurance, etc.

It is, however, between current assets and current liabilities that one of the most important comparisons lies. In the example given, not only is the ratio between the two low (1.4), but it is readily obvious that all the current liabilities are for cash. They are purchases from printers and other suppliers, unpaid authors royalties, taxation, and so forth, which may not be due for settlement at the time of casting the accounts, but which eventually will have to be paid in cash. Some 60 per cent of the current *assets*, however, are not in cash at all, but in the form of unsold stock value, which cannot be used to settle the company's liabilities until it has first been converted into cash by being sold.

The first practical conclusion to draw from this set of accounts, therefore, is that unless the stock is both quick-selling and conservatively valued, and unless good credit facilities are available to the company from its suppliers, the company will be facing considerable cash-flow difficulty at the time of these accounts; even though, provided its asset values are well founded, it is 'sound' financially. What one wishes to see in the current assets section of a publisher's balance-sheet is a high ratio of debtors to stock as compared with liabilities, though on the other hand if the debtors are high in relation to annual sales, this may cast doubts on the security of those debtors under normal customer-credit terms.

There is further use to be made of this page of the accounts in conjuction with the second part, the trading and profit and loss account, to which we therefore turn.

Trading and profit and loss account

1. Since this page represents the complete business history of the company in the period under review, it is of direct interest for the comparison of separate results, both one with another, and each with the corresponding result for the previous year. Perhaps only the final net profit figure is of interest in isolation from the rest of the results.

2. Comparisons to be made on the trading account are:

   (a) Each figure with that for the previous period in whatever depth is required, in order to isolate and control disproportionate increases.
   (b) Percentage increases in each main head of cost (manufacturing and overheads) over the previous period with the equivalent percentage increase in sales.
   (c) The percentage increase in stock value with the sales increase.

(d) The gross profit as a percentage of sales compared with the previous period.

3. The cash-flow result can be derived by excluding the stock value increase from the credit side of the page. In this example, the stock value increase is some £7000, before a net profit of £2200. After tax on the profit, therefore, the cash-flow shortfall is nearly £6000 on the year's trading, reinforcing the impression received from the balance-sheet page. This company is having to do a lot of juggling from month to month to pay its bills on time.

The accounts as a whole

There are four business ratios which are most commonly used to assess the status of a company.

1. Return on capital employed; the capital employed is usually taken to be the total of the balance-sheet liabilities, less the trade creditors and sundries. In this example, the post-tax profit of some £1200 represents a return of roughly $4\frac{1}{2}$ per cent on the employed capital of £26,000—not impressive, and less so when the high proportion of stock on the credit side of the trading account is remembered.

2. Profit on total assets employed: £1200 on £70,000 is 1·7 per cent —dismal.

3. Profit on turnover: £1200 on £137,000 is 0·9 per cent—even more dismal.

4. Turnover of assets employed: $\dfrac{£137,000}{£70,000}$ is just under 2 times.

Although this example of a publisher's balance-sheet is fictitious, nevertheless the results of analysis which it reveals may not be too far removed from the real-life situations of some book-publishing companies. The figures given disclose a number of things about the management of the company, and allow certain general *business*, as against *financial*, conclusions to be drawn.

1. The financial results are very poor, whatever criterion of analysis is employed.

2. The stock value is far too high in relation to sales revenue, although the gross profit of 40 per cent on sales is not exceptionally low. This suggests:

(a) Either that the pricing policy of the company's publications is too conservative, and should be re-examined to increase both the costing factor on new books and to raise the prices of back list titles at regular intervals, or that the overhead structure is overweight in relation to trading volume.

(b) Volume sales are sluggish, though this may be over-emphasised by underpricing.

3. The 50 per cent increase in production expenditure during the 1970 period is matched by only 35 per cent increase in sales. Is the stockbuilding excessive, or will it have a dynamic effect on the profits for 1971?

4. Staff wages have risen by 40 per cent. This may be the result of advance gearing for considerable expansion in 1971, or it may be the result of management indifference and lack of dynamism.

5. On the basis of this set of accounts, the company's future depends heavily on the results in 1971. It is short of cash, yet investing quite heavily in new publications and in staff, its total stock value is high in relation to the level of trade, and at this stage, only the detailed forecasts of 1971 revenue and expenditure will show whether its present position represents a deliberate preparation for sizeable expansion, or a company which is winding slowly downwards towards inanition and insolvency.

PROFIT MEASUREMENT

Profit for a publishing firm is a somewhat ambiguous concept, as will have been deduced from Chapter 2. Because the profit is variable according to the value placed on unsold stock, the factor most carefully to be considered is for what purpose profit is declared at all.

The profit in the balance-sheet is dependent to a surprising degree on the over- or under-valuation of stock—exact valuation is impossible. Even in educational publishing where future textbook sales can be forecast with some accuracy, and storage charges and rebinding costs can be carefully estimated, the result of any valuation made in advance remains as speculative as the outcome of a political election. Until the votes are cast (or the books sold) you do not know definitely whether the evidence you have is reliable.

There are two most common methods of valuing stock—either by a fixed percentage write-down from cost or previous year's valuation, or by a title-by-title assessment of sales over a likely life period. In the former, the method of valuation remains constant. Title-by-title valuation, however, allows the publisher to alter his assessment each year if unexpected circumstances arise which have an effect on sales of any title.

Reasons for maximising the profit may be as follows:

Capital gains or outside investment

In the event that the publisher might wish in the future to sell out his business interest, either to a bigger publishing firm or to an industrial conglomerate, or may need to take in outside investment to finance expansion, the terms of sale (or investment) will almost certainly be geared to the profit record and to the firm's net assets. The usual criterion for assessing a purchase price is the price/earnings basis—that is to say by valuing each share at so many times the net post-tax profit per share. Investment is contemplated in the same way by first establishing a value for the firm on a price/earnings basis and then formulating from that the terms of the proposed investment.

The uncertainty lies, of course, in the factor used to multiply earnings in order to obtain the eventual price. The purchaser will wish to use a low factor, the seller a high one. The factor used in any particular circumstance will depend on which is the more eager party, the buyer or the seller. Longmans, Green & Co. was sold to Lord Cowdray's industrial group in 1968 on a p/e ratio of 26—a high figure for publishing, and reflecting the strength of Longmans' bias towards educational books and materials. For small private companies, a factor of five times earnings is fairly widely accepted as the median; but it is worth remembering that the identity of the purchaser can be important, for if it is a broadly similar but larger publishing firm, the selling company may be integrated into its existing operation at a considerable overhead saving, which the seller can use as argument for a higher p/e ratio.

The greater the profit, therefore, in a steadily expanding record of not less than three years, the higher the likely price of a sale.

To establish trade confidence

It is self-evident that printers and other suppliers granting extended credit will want to be sure that the firm is financially sound enough to warrant the risk. So too will the bank manager when he is invited each year to renew or increase the overdraft. Profit growth commensurate with increases in turnover will show such interested parties that the company's margins are not under attack, and that their confidence in their customer's financial standing can be maintained.

Balancing the advantages of profit declarations against the disadvantages must be a matter of individual judgement each year, but it must now be said that, notwithstanding the foregoing, a sense of proportion is necessary about the flexibility available in valuing stocks. The Inland Revenue insist on a 'true' or 'fair' valuation, and the margin of flexibility lies only between the publisher's optimism and pessimisim about future sales of existing titles, and the consequent value of their stock at the end of a year. Nor is it possible or desirable to skip year by year from optimism to pessimism and back again. Reasonable consistency in valuing is looked for, and it is best for the publisher to formulate a general valuation policy which can be maintained from year to year, with minor adjustments as one title or another exceeds or falls behind expectation. In general, writing off all sheet stock completely and bound stock by 50 per cent annually should err sufficiently on the side of caution to avoid cash-flow difficulties over taxation on the stock portion of annual profits.

The main thing for the publisher to remember is the essential difference between the balance-sheet profit and the surplus of cash from revenue over expenditure which is in the bank or on the sales ledger. Provided all the estimating and administration is concerned with the latter, the former will reasonably take care of itself.

TAXATION CONTROL

Capital gains tax

The attraction of tax under this head is dependent upon sale of all or part of the equity or untaxed assets of the firm, and the level of taxation (1970) is 30 per cent. Control therefore takes the form of restricting the moneys received from sales of equity or assets, and increasing the amount to be paid for already taxed earnings. No great switch can be made, because reduction of equity or asset value also reduces the price/earnings ratio. But one useful device is for the directors to award themselves remuneration which is high in relation to the total profit and leave undrawn in the firm that part of the remuneration which they do not immediately need for themselves. Although income tax is payable on all such remuneration, at rates higher than 30 per cent, a price/earnings ratio can be formulated with a prospective purchaser on the profit *before* director's remuneration, yielding the same eventual purchase price, but leaving a larger part of it payable in settlement of the firm's liabilities to directors on which income tax has been paid. For example, on sale of the firm, £2000 of tax-paid undrawn director's remuneration is settled as £2000. An additional £2000 left as profit to inflate the p/e ratio attracts, if a factor of five times is used, tax of 30 per cent on the £10,000 value.

Corporation tax

Currently 40 per cent of net profit after two recent reductions, the principal way of avoiding the attraction of corporation tax is for the directors to award themselves as much of the profit in remuneration as is permissible up to the point at which their individual liabilities to income tax and surtax (their 'marginal rates') exceed 40 per cent.

Income tax

The more of the publisher's personal expenditure that can legitimately be settled by the firm on his behalf the better, because where the item is not exactly quantifiable in money terms—for example, the division of rent and rates between office and home in a joint set of premises—although the publisher is liable to taxation on a 'taxable benefit', the Inland Revenue might be persuaded to accept a division less weighted against the individual and more against the firm than the comparable market price of a similar item.

All taxation is, at best, a nuisance, but the inevitable price of society. It is foolish to seek to evade taxation, but perfectly reasonable to poke about, with the aid of a qualified accountant, among the hotch-potch of tax legislation to determine legal ways of avoiding the incidence of tax.

MANAGEMENT CONTROLS

A very large area of management science is devoted to the numerous systems of control which have been developed by practitioners and academics to promote the efficiency of industry. Efficiency—the more economical use of resources—is the forerunner of profit.

For small businesses a less scientific view may be adopted of theoretical systems like critical path analysis, discounted cash-flow analysis, and the like. In a small firm where the staff is small, and the compass of the operation is contained within a very few 'managers', the techniques of, primarily, job control, concentrate themselves more narrowly into a financial (rather than labour) context. Thus the benefit of formal control systems is reduced more or less entirely to their effect on the financial administration, and this means the reduction of the divergence between financial forecasts and financial outturn. There are a number of entirely practical methods which can be utilised, and the first to be discussed is the ordinary accounting system which the publisher will install, for this is literally a 'control'.

Sales ledger, bought ledger and stock accounting

The accounting system needed in a small publishing firm is pretty rudimentary. There are three separate areas of accounting—sales ledger, bought ledger and author's ledger. A fourth, providing for monthly trial balances to measure performance against forecast (a nominal ledger), is discussed below.

The sales ledger is a record of who has bought what value of goods from the firm. From it are required the sales revenue figures, arranged in two separate and distinct ways—chronologically by date of sale, and alphabetically by customer—so that it can reveal both the amount of trade in a day, or a week or a month, and the amount of trade done with a particular customer. The components of the system, therefore, are: a copy of the sales invoice, a 'day book' in which invoices are listed day by day, and a ledger arranged by customer, to which invoice totals are debited from the day book. When a customer pays an invoice by cheque, the reverse process takes place, through a 'cash book', in which payments are listed day by day, and from which the amounts of each payment are posted to credit the customer's account in the sales ledger.

The bought ledger is run on exactly the same system as the sales ledger, except that it controls purchases by the publisher from his suppliers, instead of sales to the publisher's customers. It is, however, unlikely that a small firm will need a full bought-ledger system. There will be only a handful of suppliers—a printer or two, a binder, blockmaker, stationery supplier, landlord and so on—perhaps no more than thirty all told, excluding authors. These accounts can be controlled from the suppliers' original invoices, which are collated together in groups according to the month in which they are to be paid, and entered as they are paid in a 'payments cash book' which has sufficient analysis columns for the payments to be analysed under the headings of expenditure used by the auditor in the profit and loss account.

The author's control does require a ledger arranged alphabetically by author, though not a separate day book, since author's royalties will be paid in batches at specific times of the year, rather than at random throughout the year. At the end of each royalty period, the amount due to each author is calculated and debited to his account in the ledger. Any advance payment to him, or books bought by him from the publisher, are credited to his account, and the balance due likewise credited when it is paid, payment being recorded also through the payment cash book in a single analysis column marked 'author'.

Also needed is a separate sales and stock record kept under title arrangement, in which copies of each book sold can be marked to provide the total of sales by title at the end of each royalty period.

Checks on out-turns

It is usual practice in most firms to take each month 'trial balances' —in effect the preparation of complete, internal accounts for trading and profit and loss, either for the month, or from the beginning of the trading period up to the latest month end. Obviously no firm can expect to operate with only year-end knowledge of how well or badly it is doing; much more frequent information is necessary.

In larger firms the trial balances will follow closely or exactly the annual accounting form, or may concentrate more heavily on specific aspects of the company's activity, production investment, sales revenue broken down by territories, and so on.

In smaller firms the formality of monthly accounts is unnecessarily arduous, but some method of control is required of main heads of revenue and expenditure, and of special items according to the particular concern at any one time. An example of the latter might be the sales performance of one particular representative about whom the management has doubts. Controls of this sort are a matter of common sense, once the necessary areas have been delineated.

The publisher needs to know from month to month both how the firm is doing in terms of profit or loss and in terms of cash flow. Some of the simple systems which can be used (and varied according to necessity) as are follows:

1. *Bought-day-book out-turn*

It has already been said that the small firm does not need to maintain a formal day book and ledger system for its purchases since the number of different suppliers is likely to be small and easily controlled through a cash book with sufficient analysis columns. Without some form of daily record of purchases, however, he cannot assess profitability from month to month.

It is sufficient for the publisher (or his accountant) to keep a loose-leaf binder with a page carrying three money columns for each month

(Fig. 8). In this, he enters as it is received, each supplier's invoice, in either the column headed 'production' or the column headed 'overhead', and added into the third column, which is the combined total of the other two. He must in addition include any payments which relate to the current month not made against supplier's invoice (e.g. cheques cashed for postage stamps or petty cash, wages cheques) and a computation at the end of the month for authors' royalties incurred on the sales during the month.

He must exclude suppliers' invoices which do not relate to the current month—for example, printers' invoices for books to be published, say, two months ahead, since these count as work in progress. If suppliers' invoices which do relate to the current month are late in arriving, then an estimate of them must be included, and any adjustment necessary when the exact amount is known can be added to the later month when the invoice is received. At the end of each month, therefore, there is a combined total of costs incurred on production and overheads during the month, which is sufficiently accurate to reveal the current level of expenditure.

Adjustments to this total in order to obtain the month's balance-sheet profit, if this is required, are three:

(a) Deduct the amount of director's actual drawings recorded on the day-book sheet to leave the result as 'pre-directors' remuneration.

(b) Add adjustments of the stock value decrease as a result of back list sales, and increase as a result of the unsold copies of the new publications charged during the month.

(c) Allow for any payments recorded which are prepayments.

Since this is intended deliberately as an informal record, it is better to avoid excessive postponement of suppliers' invoices for work-in-progress. Thus the printing, binding and paper costs of a new book can be carried forward to the appropriate month of publication, but small costs, such as jacket design fees or blockmaking charges, are more conveniently entered in the day book when they are received. If a record sheet of production costs is kept for each individual title, as is necessary for costing purposes, it is simple to

FIG. 8. BOUGHT-DAY-BOOK—COSTS ATTRIBUTABLE TO JUNE

Date		Production and royalty		Overheads		Total	
		£	p	£	p	£	p
1	Back list title reprint	484	0			484	0
1	June new publications—printing	1103	25			1587	25
2	Cash			60	0	1647	25
3	Postage stamps bought			10	25	1657	50
	Overseas bulk post a/c			13	30	1670	80
6	Stationery			3	24	1674	4
8	Postage stamps			29	50	1703	54
	Cash			10	0	1713	54
	Additional NHI stamp			2	48	1716	2
	Stationery			1	70	1717	72
11	Cash			65	0	1782	72
12	Overseas cable charge				92	1783	64
14	Postage stamps			16	50	1800	14
18	Cash			65	0	1865	14
	Editorial reader's fee			5	25	1870	39
19	Leather binding presentation copy	5	87			1876	26
	Postage stamps			19	50	1895	76
21	Cash			10	0	1905	76
22	Address costs for mailing shot			105	30	2011	6
	June new publication—printing	817	20			2828	26
23	Cash			60	0	2888	26
	Stationery			9	27	2897	53
26	June salaries, NHI, PAYE, etc.			369	49	3267	2
	Postage stamps			19	75	3286	77
27	Gas board a/c			13	81	3300	58
	Mailing shot postage			114	86	3415	44
30	Bank charges April/June (estimate)			45	0	3460	44
	Quarterly rent in arrears			300	0	3760	44
	June new publications—binding	755	50			4515	94
	Stationery			14	65	4529	59
	Printed stationery			7	62	4537	21
	Author royalties on June sales	671	51			5208	27
		3837	33	1371	39	5208	27

abstract form it prepayments made for such items on unpublished books.

The actual day-book sheet may look as casual as the illustration above (Fig. 8), but the information it embodies is deceptively important and will be used in two ways: for comparison with the overhead forecast, and for consolidation into the monthly trading analysis (see Fig. 10).

2. *Bought-day-book forecast*

Budget forecasting has already been discussed earlier in this chapter. A simple form suffices, when operational, for checking outturn against forecast. The form (Fig. 9) itemises different heads of expenditure, and provides a monthly 'norm' for each head, with columns in which expenditure can be abstracted from the bought-day-book sheet for comparison with the norm. The important proviso to this is that month-by-month comparisons are invalid on the brief form shown; with items like rent payable quarterly, and catalogue mailing every half-year, this form is suitable only for the comparison of quarterly or half-yearly totals. Separate breakdowns of the expenditure heads must be made if more detailed comparisons are required, in the manner of the budgeting chart shown on page 81.

3. *Monthly trading analysis*

This group of results acts as a form of balance-sheet, without, however, the detailed breakdown of expenditure heads.

The form shown (Fig. 10) contains four groups of figures on a monthly basis: sales revenue (broken down into home and export), cash book revenue and expenditure, day-book expenditure, and profit. The amount of the debtors' ledger is obtained by deducting cash received from sales revenue, the surplus remaining outstanding on the ledger. The profit is obtained by deducting the bought-day-book total from sales revenue. To convert the resultant figure into balance-sheet profit, once again add back directors' actual drawings and adjust for stock value alterations, bad debt expectations and prepayments charged during the month.

This very simple set of forms, which it is neither arduous nor complex to maintain, thus gives a very comprehensive picture of the state of the business at each month's end. There is no reason why the forms should not be kept on a weekly, or even daily, basis if the need for financial knowledge is sufficiently fanatical.

4. *Payments control*

Although the bought-ledger figures in the monthly trading analysis give some general indication of the budgeting necessary for month-

FIG. 9. OVERHEADS—CHECKS ON OUT-TURN

Item	Norm	Variations						Total variations
		July	Aug.	Sept.	Oct.	Nov.	Dec.	
Petty cash inc. wages	220	+20	−25	+80	+20			
Salaries	160	−5	+54	−4	+15			
Directors' drawings	250	−20	−20	—	+100			
Stamps inc. bulk postage	110	+9	−40	+1	+3			
Bulk mailing shots—postage	50	−50	−50	−50	−50			
NHI	50	—	+12	−1	−1			
PAYE	110	+17	−9	−1	−28			
Casual labour	15	−15	−15	−15	−15			
Rent and rates	120	−120	−120	+180	−9			
Telephone, electricity, gas	30	−30	+47	−27	−48			
Stationery	30	+6	+14	−8	−30			
Packing materials	30	−30	−30	−30	−30			
Agents' commissions	15	+47	−15	−15	+23			
Insurances	20	+80	+97	−20	−20			
Bank charges	20	−18	−18	+25	−23			
Publicity and advertising	15	+90	−15	+15	+9			
Catalogue and leaflet printings	50	+266	−50	−50	−50			
Travel	10	+19	+15	+27	—			
Running total		+266	−162	+107	−134			
			+104	+211	+77			

Fig. 10. Monthly Trading Summaries, 1970/71

SALES

	Home				Export				Total			
	£	p	£	p	£	p	£	p	£	p	£	p
July	2337	60	2337	60	2777	5	2777	5	5114	65	5114	65
Aug.	2667	80	5005	40	4476	45	7253	50	7144	25	12,258	90
Sept.	3046	20	8051	60	2665	20	9918	70	5711	40	17,970	30
Oct.	3824	30	11,875	90	2698	37	12,617	7	6522	67	24,492	97
Nov.												
Dec.												
Jan.												
Feb.												
Mar.												
April												
May												
June												

CASH BOOK

	Cash received				Cash paid out				Debtors			
	£	p	£	p	£	p	£	p	£	p	£	p
July	4431	58	4431	58	3651	15	3651	15	17,613	89		
Aug.	2669	79	7101	37	4909	20	8560	35	+683	7	18,296	96
Sept.	4520	42	11,621	79	3601	10	12,161	45	+4474	46	22,771	42
Oct.	4996	83	16,618	62	4161	75	16,323	20	+1190	98	23,962	40
Nov.									+1525	84	25,488	24
Dec.												
Jan.												
Feb.												
Mar.												
April												
May												
June												

BOUGHT LEDGER

	Production and Royalty				Overheads				Total				Surplus	
July	4186	6	4186	6	1709	13	1709	13	5895	19	5895	19	−780	53
Aug.	3180	41	7366	48	1137	30	2846	42	4317	71	10,212	90	+2046	0
Sept.	3073	13	10,439	61	1412	54	4258	96	4485	67	19,698	57	+3271	74
Oct.	5477	65	15,917	26	1169	87	5428	83	6647	52	21,344	9	+3146	89
Nov.														
Dec.														
Jan.														
Feb.														
Mar.														
April														
May														
June														

end payments to suppliers, detailed control is most simply effected over the actual invoices, which can be scheduled for payment as they arrive and clipped together in monthly batches, together with a standard form showing the non-invoice payments expected to be made each month. Unless the company has an unusually large number of suppliers, manual control of up to thirty invoices, and perhaps half that number of non-invoice payments, is very easy. It is, however, necessary as each month progresses to compare outstanding payments against receipts, perhaps from week to week, so that if the latter fall below target or expectation, rescheduling of payments can be carried out as necessary.

5. *Sales forecasting*

Methods of sales forecasting must perforce vary from firm to firm, according both to the nature of the books published and the experience available within a firm of past results. Most methods boil down simply to common-sense appraisals of how many copies of which titles will be sold within what period, and the accuracy of these depends, subjectively, on the forecaster.

Another technical device, however, which I have not seen used elsewhere, depends on a correlation between the published prices of new books and the sales revenue to be derived from them in constant circumstances concerning the subject matter of the publishing programme, the costing structure, and other points. It is as shown in Fig. 11.

Subject to some provisos, it seems that there may be a chartable correlation between the total of published prices of a firm's output and the firm's sales revenue (turnover) during a given period. It may be possible in certain cases to use the correlations of several periods (say, years) as a starting-point for sales forecasting, but this is of course no substitute for a sales budget by title.

The most important proviso, of course, is that if any statistic of one year's publishing operation is to be related for comparative or speculative purposes to the same statistic of another year, there should be no significant change in the general nature of the publishing operation. Thus the pricing policy and the kind of output must have

FIG. 11. PRICE/TURNOVER RELATIONSHIP

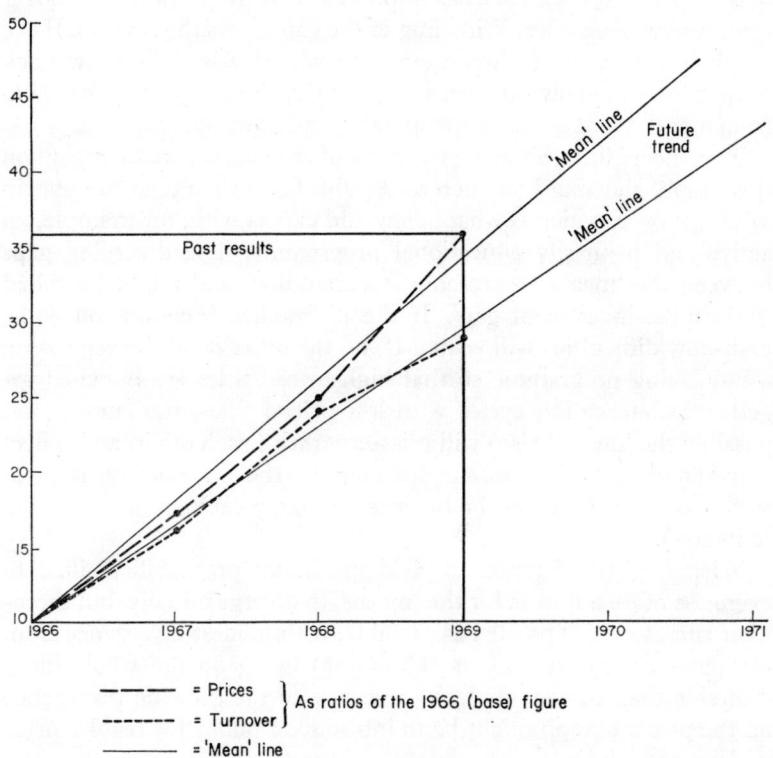

```
         = Prices   ⎫
                    ⎬ As ratios of the 1966 (base) figure
         = Turnover ⎭
         = 'Mean' line
```

remained roughly the same; the latter need not be confined to specialist fields of publishing, provided the same general balance between the different subject areas has been maintained (i.e. the proportions of general fiction, to literary fiction, to general non-fiction, to educational, etc.).

Represented on the graph (Fig. 11) are lines for the total of published prices of books issued by an imaginary firm, and the sales turnover obtained, for each of the years 1966 to 1969. They are expressed as ratios, using in each case the 1966 figure as the base (10). The two main lines follow parabolic curves, and the instance where the curves move towards each other, narrowing the gaps between them, reflects a period in which back-list sales improved their proportion of turnover against new book sales. Widening of the gap shows the reverse. If the graph is plotted on a three-monthly basis, this back list:new book proportion can show up even more clearly, though price imbalances from month to month are correspondingly distorting.

The 'mean' lines, showing the *trend* of each curve, are divergent on this graph, showing how increased published prices tend to outstrip sales turnover, which is what one would expect with, for example, an active and primarily educational programme. The diverging gaps between the 'means' represents stockbuilding, and might be called 'the capital-investment gap'. If the divergence becomes too wide, cash-flow difficulties will ensue. If, on the other hand, by regulating a publishing programme so that high-priced titles are bunched together in alternating cycles with low-priced titles, the curves (and possibly the 'means' also) will criss-cross with each other, and reflect corresponding periods of surplus and shortfall in capacity, both of staff and of cash (unless the business is highly capitalised in relation to its size).

What ought to happen to yield maximum profitability allied to evenness of cash flow is for the 'means' to diverge initially, but thereafter run as closely parallel as possible, with modest divergence from the parallel (representing stockbuilding) being on the whole more desirable than convergence. A corrective to the growing divergence on the present graph might be to introduce a policy for regular price reviews of back-list titles.

This kind of graph is not suggested as a prime tool in financial forecasting, but for anyone running a consistent type of publishing operation, it can provide some useful general data when reviewing past results or planning future targets.

Lastly, Fig. 12 shows a 'profit' chart which I compiled some years ago, showing the percentage profit to be derived from various permutations of overhead cost and sales volume. It is a general yardstick only, though the figures shown are mathematically correct. A star in the extreme right-hand column indicates that the venture cannot break even on that permutation.

1 AVERAGE TRADE DISCOUNT GIVEN Percentage of published price	2 AUTHOR'S ROYALTY Percentage of published price	3 OFFICE OVERHEAD Percentage of turnover	4 'TIMES' FIGURE	5 UNIT PRODUCTION COST Percentage of published price	6 NET PROFIT IF EDITION SELLS OUT ALL COPIES Percentage on turnover	7–8 NET PROFIT PERCENTAGE ON TURNOVER IF ¾ OF THE EDITION IS SOLD		9–10 NET PROFIT PERCENTAGE ON TURNOVER IF ⅔ OF THE EDITION IS SOLD		11–12 NET PROFIT PERCENTAGE ON TURNOVER IF ½ OF THE EDITION IS SOLD		13 PERCENTAGE OF THE EDITION WHICH MUST BE SOLD IN ORDER TO BREAK EVEN ON THE VENTURE
						INCLUDING STOCK VALUE	EXCLUDING STOCK VALUE	INCLUDING STOCK VALUE	EXCLUDING STOCK VALUE	INCLUDING STOCK VALUE	EXCLUDING STOCK VALUE	
40	10	33⅓	3½	28⅔	2½	2½	−13½	2½	−21½	2½	−45	95
			4	25	8½	8½	−5½	8½	−12½	8½	−33⅓	83½
			4½	22⅓	12¾	12¾	½	12¾	−5½	12¾	−24	74½
			5	20	16⅔	16⅔	5½	16⅔	—	16⅔	−16⅔	66⅔
		40	3½	28⅔	−4¼	−4¼	−20	−4¼	−28	−4¼	−52	•
			4	25	1⅔	1⅔	−12	1⅔	−19	1⅔	−40	96
			4½	22⅓	6	6	−6½	6	−12	6	−31	85
			5	20	10	10	−1	10	−6½	10	−23	77
	12½	33⅓	3½	28⅔	−2	−2	−18	−2	−25	−2	−50	•
			4	25	4	4	−10	4	−16⅔	4	−37½	91
			4½	22⅓	8½	8½	−3½	8½	−10	8½	−28	81
			5	20	12½	12½	1	12½	−4	12½	−21	73
		40	3½	28⅔	−8½	−8½	−24	−8½	−32½	−8½	−56	•
			4	25	−2½	−2½	−16	−2½	−23	−2½	−44	•
			4½	22⅓	2	2	−10	2	−16	2	−35	94½
			5	20	6	6	−5	6	−10	6	−27½	85
45	10	33⅓	3½	28⅔	−3½	−3½	−21	−3½	−29½	−3½	−55½	•
			4	25	3	3	−12	3	−20	3	−42½	94
			4½	22⅓	8	8	−5	8	−12	8	−32½	83
			5	20	12	12	—	12	−6½	12	−24	75
		40	3½	28⅔	−10	−10	−27	−10	−36	−10	−62	•
			4	25	−3½	−3½	−19	−3½	−26	−3½	−49	•
			4½	22⅓	1½	1½	−12	1½	−19	1½	−39	96½
			5	20	5½	5½	−6½	5½	−13	5½	−31	87
	12½	33⅓	3½	28⅔	−8	−8	−25	−8	−34	−8	−60	•
			4	25	−1½	−1½	−16⅔	−1½	−24	−1½	−47	•
			4½	22⅓	3½	3½	−10	3½	−16⅔	3½	−37	92
			5	20	7½	7½	−4½	7½	−10½	7½	−29	83
		40	3½	28⅔	−15	−15	−32	−15	−41	−15	−66⅔	•
			4	25	−8	−8	−23	−8	−32	−8	−53½	•
			4½	22⅓	−3½	−3½	−16⅔	−3½	−23	−3½	−43	•
			5	20	1	1	−11	1	−17	1	−35	97½

It is worth re-emphasising, in conclusion, the nature and purpose of control systems. They are checks upon the efficiency of an industrial operation—on its forecasting, achievement and servicing. Servicing controls, which apply primarily to labour activities, are relevant in larger organisations, but less so in small ones. Checks on the accuracy of determinable forecasts and performances, especially financial, are necessary in any size of organisation. They are tools of management, even in the mainly obvious and unsophisticated forms shown above, intended to improve management's knowledge of the industrial operation, and to be instituted to fill specific gaps only in that knowledge, in the most simple mode of operation compatible with their efficient use.

CHAPTER 4

METHOD—2. OPERATIONAL

THERE are three main divisions of the publishing operation—into editorial, production, and sales. In describing the activities of each of these divisions I must acknowledge that part of the factual substance of this chapter appeared originally in my earlier book, *Book Publishing Practice*, published in 1966 by Crosby Lockwood & Son Ltd. (to whom thanks are due for permission to re-use material) and now out of print.

EDITORIAL

The editor's job falls into three categories: advance planning of a publishing programme, obtaining material for publication, and editorial work on manuscripts.

Advance planning

Because of the length of time which the physical production of a book takes—seldom less than six months, sometimes as much as two years—any publishing firm which does not entirely rely on the submission of completed manuscripts as its source of material is obliged to plan its programmes, at least on a provisional basis, for a period not less than eight months in advance, and running ahead up to three or four years in some cases. The speculative nature of this necessity can present difficulties, for planning must be done according to the firm's general criteria for future expansion, for development of particular areas of a list and so on, and it is seldom possible to be sure what books will arrive in the office on any future date, whether commissioned or unsolicited, and whether they will be in a publishable state, or vary considerably in length and scope from the specification which a commissioned author promised at the time of signing his contract. Flexibility is obligatory, over and above a firm base of scheduled future publications which can be added to or reduced as circumstances may later demand, without damaging or straining the resources of the firm and its financial and trading objectives.

The editor has, therefore, to spend a considerable amount of time searching out and arranging for the future delivery of books which may not be published for several years ahead, and fitting them provisionally into a future publishing schedule. In my own company we have a 'full' programme scheduled for about eighteen months forward publishing (not a long time), which may be adjusted as much as a dozen times before the period is reached, as books drop out for one reason or another, and/or new titles are offered which can be written or published quickly. One of the most important principles in planning the forward programme is to ensure a reasonably constant growth of the total published prices projected for each publication date (providing regular turnover prospects month by month), and numerical evenness of the programme from month to month so that warehousing and dispatch resources are not overstrained by having to cope with, say, six new titles on one date, and a single title on the next.

Obtaining material for publication

Although popular belief has it that publishers merely sit in their offices and wait to be inundated with wonderful manuscripts, not only is this not the case, but often the very opposite happens. Publishers who publish only in a special subject field hardly ever accept unsolicited books. They prefer to commission from suitable authors the books which their technical advisers recommend as necessary. In general publishing, acceptance of an unsolicited manuscript is comparatively rare, especially a novel or volume of poetry. Of the 100,000 or so would-be authors writing books in Britain at any one time, less than 5 per cent are destined to see print. The main reason for this is that the remainder are judged substandard. There are occasional books on subjects so obscure that no publisher can turn them into commercial propositions, but the failures of these are few and far between, not least because of a thriving university-press section of British publishing which is prepared to publish works of scholarship irrespective of their purely commercial prospects. But whoever originated the phrase that every man has one book inside him was clearly possessed of too much imagination and too little judgement. Yet in 1969, 31,416 book titles were published in Britain, a number of them being new editions and reprints of existing works, and others importations in finished form from other countries. They reach their publishers in one of four different ways: as a result of the publisher's commission, from a literary agent, sent unsolicited by authors, or bought ready-made or in the form of rights from an overseas publisher.

Direct commissions. The majority of technical and educational books are commissioned from their authors by the publisher, either by the latter making the first approach to the former with a subject-brief arranged which the publisher or his advisers know will fill a gap in the literature or take advantage of a particular marketing situation; or else by the publisher accepting a proposed book brought to him in outline and giving the author a contract to write it. Commissions may from time to time be given for non-technical books—on topics of current but perhaps ephemeral interest, such as a general election battle—and almost always for biographies.

Literary agents. The literary agent is an entrepreneur who acts on an author's behalf in the selling of a manuscript or an article, a film scenario or any piece of commercial writing to a publisher. Literary agents take their commission, usually 10–15 per cent, depending on what rights they have sold, from the author's share of revenue produced by the piece of writing. They are very much a twentieth-century phenomenon whose businesses depend on personal contact, on the ability to attract author customers to themselves, and then to sell their wares to the publishing trade and to films and broadcasting.

There is no doubt whatever that authors are in general very much better off as a result of literary agency, even though three-quarters of published books probably still earn less than £500 for their authors. Good agents, who must have a highly developed ability to evaluate all forms of literary composition, can nevertheless earn for their authors sums which the authors could seldom expect to obtain for themselves. Agents also act as a buffer between author and publisher, especially valuable where an author lacks business sense and a publisher, with a too acute commercial instinct, may not scruple to trade on the fact. Literary agents are also becoming accepted by publishers as useful providers of suitable authors for specific commissions.

Although the agency business developed in general and non-academic writing, the growth of educational literature has seen several agencies in recent years setting up departments to act on behalf of academic authors. One of the ancillary services of an agent is to advise on the wise disposition and investment of large-scale earnings from writings, which can make him of special value to the author of a wide-selling standard textbook. To the authors of more run-of-the-mill works, an agent's fee may seem superfluous unless the author is especially dubious about the nature of the relationship upon which he is embarking with his publisher. I cannot in my own case conceive of additional concessions in our terms to our authors which an agent might obtain for an author that he could not himself obtain from us by a reasoned argument. But I admit to a personal bias against agents as the result of the demands with which I was sometimes faced from them when I worked in a general publishing house.

Unsolicited manuscripts. Over the whole range of present-day publishing it is never less than unusual for a complete and unsolicited manuscript to be accepted for publication. An unsolicited manuscript nine times out of ten denotes an unpublished author, for publishers tend to hang on to the authors they publish and to keep close tabs on their further work, and authors themselves, once published, are understandably inclined to sell future works, or the ideas of them, before embarking upon the labour of writing. Occasionally a book contracted for may be rejected when it is completed, and therefore land on another publisher's desk, but it takes considerable optimism, as well as stamina, to engage in the construction of a book, with absolutely no assurance of its ever being published.

Foreign imports. The English language is the most powerful marketing weapon available to publishers. It is the principal tongue of the U.K., U.S.A., Australasia and certain parts of the Commonwealth, and the alternative or second language in Canada, South Africa, India and many other countries, embracing a total population of hundreds of millions of people.

The exchange of publications between countries of the same language is highly developed—through sales of territory publishing rights for titles of reasonable market potential, especially general books, and through sales from one country to another of finished copies, either in very small quantities, or in editions, with the importing publisher's imprint, of, say, 500 or 1000 copies. In education, in particular, the methods of one country may not accord sufficiently with those in another to make a textbook 'standard' in both, but it may nevertheless be of peripheral subject interest in the country of import. In general, cross-purchases are pursued with equal vigour by exporters and importers.

Author contracts

Whether a book is the publisher's idea and commissioned from an author or whether it comes from an author or an agent, the publisher's contract is likely to contain much the same sort of terms. It is in all cases the author who must sign it. Agents are not generally empowered to sign contracts on their authors' behalf.

The contract for a book is usually a complex document. It covers the leasing of certain important rights in a work, and the extent of the lease and the protective conditions which limit it are hardly less varied than the provisions of a lease for a house or flat. The contract starts off with a set legal formula identifying the signatories and saying what the agreement is about. The first material clause is devoted to the territory in which the publisher is to be allowed to publish the book, and a general statement of the rights he is accorded by the contract. There are three different 'territorial' areas of the world for the purposes of publishing, and one of these is not geographical but linguistic. The areas are the British Commonwealth market, the traditional American market—both of them for English language books— and the whole world in translated languages.

The minimum territory usually accepted by a British publisher from an author is the British Empire and Commonwealth as constituted at 1st January, 1947, the date of the former British Empire Market Agreement, now known as the British Publishers' Traditional Market Agreement. This represents the British Commonwealth as it is today, plus such former members and protected territories as South Africa and Kuwait. The traditional American market in which an American publisher will be licensed to publish the book quite independently of British arrangements is the United States with or without Canada (a bone of frequent contention) and American trust or acknowledged territories such as the Philippine Islands. The rest of the world is neither granted to nor withheld from the publisher of the English language edition, but is usually designated an 'open market', meaning that anyone may distribute his edition. The extent of the market accorded by an author is, of course, subject to negotiation. A publisher who is commissioning a book of his own devising may insist on retaining control of world publishing rights and all translation rights. At other times an author or his agent may offer only the barest minimum, and retain as much as possible to sell direct elsewhere. The minimum rights which the Publishers Association recommends its members to accept are full volume rights—that is all rights to publish in book form whether in hard covers or paperback binding. The subsidiary rights which may accompany volume rights are detailed later in this chapter.

Having stated the rights which are granted and the territories in which they may be exercised, the contract then turns to the payment (the 'consideration') which the publisher is to make for them and the supplementary conditions which attach both to the rights and to the book which is the subject of the contract.

Payment to the author is in the dual form of a royalty calculated on the published price of sales of the publisher's edition of the book and an agreed proportion of revenues received for lease of any subsidiary rights to another publisher. Occasionally a contract may provide for the publisher to receive from the author some of the revenue from subsidiary rights which the author has retained and sold on his own account. This is uncommon, and occurs only in cases where the author is ready to concede either that it is due to publication of his book that he has been able to sell the particular subsidiary right which has brought in the revenue, or else that by selling the right, for example to a book club, he has hindered sales of the publisher's edition in the territory which the publisher has been granted. Royalty payments to authors usually begin at 10 per cent of the published price on United Kingdom sales and 5 per cent on sales overseas (where the publisher may have to meet higher agents' commission, an additional wholesaler's share and higher terms demanded by local booksellers). Well-known authors may command a higher royalty, but 10 per cent as a starting figure is widely accepted, although a publisher may offer a sliding scale of royalty, increasing as sales of the book increase. In any firm there is only a fixed percentage of the published prices of books which is available for payment to the authors. Any excess promised means an increase in the price of the book, and if an author or agent insists on a high royalty percentage he cannot then blame an uncompetitive published price for a book's subsequent failure. By asking for a higher royalty an author, not as a rule a highly paid member of society, is effectively requesting an increased share of his publisher's net profit margin.

Subsidiary rights income, which has increased out of all proportion since the war, derives mainly from the sale or lease of paperback reprint rights, serial and one-shot newspaper periodical rights and, of course, foreign edition and translation rights. The small sums available from permissions to anthologise or quote small sections of a book are usually divided equally between author and publisher. Revenue from paperback rights, to a share of which the publisher defends his claim on the two grounds already mentioned, has hitherto been split equally, but this arrangement is coming under increased pressure for the author to receive a 60 per cent share. First or pre-publication serial rights do not carry the claim that it is the publisher's edition which has made their sale possible, and only occasionally will an agent concede the publisher a courtesy 10 per cent. Post-publication serial rights usually yield the publisher one-third of their revenue, and if first, second and subsequent serial and syndication rights are sold together as a 'package deal' to one buyer an astute publisher may be able to arrange to receive 15–25 per cent of the revenue. Under an agent's contract he is unlikely to share to any significant extent in revenue from either translation rights or English-language rights in territories outside his own.

Where, however, the book is commissioned by the publisher as his own idea he will endeavour to ensure that he retains complete control of all possible rights in the book, though as an honest publisher anxious to retain both reputation and authors, he will doubtless be ready to divide all his rights income equally with the author.

Proceeds, as far as the author is concerned, do not normally materialise until pretty late in the day. The custom has therefore evolved of paying authors an advance against *expected* earnings either upon signature of the contract, completion of the manuscript or publication of the book. The custom originated in the need to keep a writer's body and soul together while he was engaged on writing the book contracted for. Today the size and time of payment are subject to far more negotiation between author and publisher than are basic royalty rates. A publisher is asked to show his faith in a book and its earning power by making a substantial advance payment, and advances are the prime method of publisher competition and the prize for which an unscrupulous agent may hold a book up to auction. The advance is likely to be the largest single sum of earnings that an unexceptional author will see from his book, and it is quite common for an advance not to be earned by royalties on sales, which effectively raises the percentage rate of royalty payment. Contracts state whether an advance is against all earnings from the book or covers only book royalties, in which case a publisher may be required to pay an author his share of subsidiary rights income immediately it is received from a purchaser.

The clauses in a contract which concern the work itself specify the length and date of delivery of the manuscript, provide for the publisher to pay all production costs except, usually, corrections to the proofs above 10 per cent of the total cost of composition (a method of ensuring that the author does not take galley proofs as a signal to commence rewriting his book) and the copyright and libel warranty.

Length of the book and delivery date are a matter of common-sense agreement. Contracts usually contain a proviso that if the author fails to deliver by the agreed date the publisher may cancel the arrangement and demand his advance back. This is more a threat than a fixed intention, and does ensure that the publisher has reasonable advance knowledge of what books to schedule for each publishing season.

The libel and copyright warranty is usually a more serious affair. In many cases a publisher cannot possibly tell whether a libel or breach of copyright has been perpetrated by an author in his book, and, alas, ignorance is no defence to an action at law under either head. A substantial sum of money is spent by publishers each year in retrieving the effects of libels published innocently by them, for although many publishers take out insurance against libel, the maximum cover obtainable is 90 per cent of the damages. Although an author cannot indemnify a publisher against the consequences of a criminal or obscene libel, for which the punishment may be a sentence of imprisonment—one man cannot go to prison in another's stead—he can undertake to reimburse the publisher for any financial loss caused by the civil torts of libel or breach of copyright in his book. It is a well-attested principle that authors should warrant against libel—the legal effect of a warranty is to give the other party to a contract the right to terminate the contract or to sue for damages if the warranty is breached—and indemnify the costs thereof. Authors, however, are usually impecunious people, and a libel warranty's purpose may have little more effect than to impress upon an author by the complexity of its phraseology the gravity of committing a libel. Many literary agents, while paying lip service to the principle of indemnity, include in their contracts with publishers a clause which totally avoids the author's responsibility unless the libel has been written intentionally into his book. The most other-worldly of authors is scarcely likely to admit in open court that he has deliberately libelled a plaintiff!

Other clauses in the contract cover such matters as authors' free copies, the dates to which the publisher shall make up royalty accounts, provision for an editor to be appointed if the author is unwilling to revise the book for a new edition, circumstances in which the rights granted to the publisher shall revert to the author (usually for breach of contract and for failure to exploit the rights, if, for instance, the book is allowed to remain out of print), some provision about who is to pay reproduction fees for illustrations, the publisher's right to remainder the edition and sometimes an option clause.

This option clause is subject to much dispute and is of doubtful legal validity. It is, candidly, no more than an attempt by the publisher to put one over on the author by insisting that he, the publisher, be given first refusal of the author's next one or two books, sometimes on the same terms as the present contract. This can be particularly unfair where the present contract covers, say, a first novel on which the terms correspond with the risk and are not very generous. Publishers defend the option clause on the ground that if they have taken the risks of launching a new author, often unprofitably, they should not submit to his being filched away by richer offers as soon as his writing becomes profitable. Literary agents fight this approach fiercely, and they are right to do so. In general, if a publisher serves his author satisfactorily the author will not desert him. If he does not, all the option clauses in the world will not produce a happy working relationship. It is not axiomatic that authors quit their first patrons just because they are offered slightly larger advances elsewhere.

Last of all the general clauses comes that covering claim to copyright, which usually states that the copyright of the book remains with the author, and the publisher shall claim it for him with the usual formula—© and the date of claim—in the preliminary pages of the book. Occasionally a publisher may demand or purchase the copyright of a book from an author, in which case the author has no further legal interest in the book or its fortunes. This, however, is rare, for ownership of the copyright conveys to a publisher no interest that cannot be granted in the licence to publish.

Editorial work on the manuscript

The mechanical process of publishing above begins with the editor. First of all, the manuscript is read through for spelling and for grammatical and factual accuracy. The editor also ensures that the manuscript is stylistically consistent. Each firm has its own house style which is adopted for all books and contains consistent rules about optional spellings—'encyclopaedia' or 'encyclopedia', 'anglicize' or 'anglicise'—single or double quotation marks, the use of capital letters, whether figures are printed as figures or spelt out in words, punctuation and whether stops are used in, say, abbreviations like H.M.S.O. or after people's initials. There are numerous possible ambiguities, a definite ruling on which goes to establish a house style. Marking up a manuscript to style is a surprisingly skilled job, particularly if the book is a well-documented text with cross references and copious footnotes. Some firms have arrangements with their printers, whereby the latter are supplied with a standard set of style instructions, and the publisher marks up only the first two or three pages of the manuscript. The printer does the rest. There exist also a number of standard guides to style, such as the *Rules for compositors and readers at the University Press, Oxford*, which may be adopted by publisher and printer, and most printers have a house style of their own which the publisher may be willing to accept.

The editor may also find it necessary to sub-edit the book—to re-write or reshape passages in the text in order to improve style or cut out verbosity. This occurs less with fiction and biography, for example, where the author is usually a writer by trade, than with practical handbooks by people more experienced with, say, a fishing rod or at a carpentry bench than with pen. Different authors permit different operations upon their manuscripts. In journalism sub-editing to editorial requirements is more common than in book publishing.

If sub-editing of a book has been heavy, the alterations should be checked with the author, since he, in the last resort, is the arbiter of his book's content. In these cases, I have myself usually experienced one of three reactions from the author: either he finds the sub-editing a gross personal affront and quite unacceptable, in which case, unless he can be persuaded to change his mind, publication of his book collapses; or he admits the sub-editing as improving on his original work; or, most common of all, we tacitly pretend that the sub-editing has not happened at all, and that the corrected script is exactly as he first submitted it!

It is my opinion that a capable editor both needs and can afford to be as tough as he likes with his authors about sub-editing. A novelist may be the best judge of aesthetics, or a scientist the expert on a matter of science, but the editor knows what he can sell, and it is his job to insist that he gets it from his authors. There can have been very few books published which have passed from author to printer in typescript without any editorial additions intervening.

PRODUCTION

The production manager controls the mechanical transformation of a typescript into a bound volume. The printer and binder who perform the actual task of setting up the book in type, printing it and casing it refer to the publisher for all production decisions, and the production manager must not only have the answer to their enquiries, he must have made almost all his decisions before the manuscript is dispatched to the printer. He has to translate the general wishes of both editorial and sales departments into visible results, and will work particularly closely with the sales department, which relies on him both to maintain a pre-selected production schedule and to provide some of the sales promotional material. The production manager is not usually a qualified graphic designer, except in those firms which specialise in books of great typographical and visual complexity. He must, however, be able to recognise quality both of design and print, and himself handle much routine typography. He has probably spent most of his working life on the production side of publishing, but this is not to say that he need not have an eye sharp enough sometimes to spot a defamatory reference or factual mistake where the editor has missed it.

The first decision which the production manager has to take when he receives the manuscript from the editor with general instructions about appearance, length of run and so on is the process he wishes to use to print the book. For practical purposes there are two processes suitable for printing books—letterpress and offset lithography. Letterpress is the process in which each letter of the type (or line) is cast in lead in a matrix, assembled into lines of type, thence into pages, and printed by impressing the inked formes containing the pages of type on to a sheet of paper passed through the printing machine. It involves three separate machine processes: first the tapping out of the text, on a keyboard not unlike an elaborate typewriter, on to a roll of paper which is perforated by the tapping mechanism; casting the type by passing the roll through the caster, where air forced through the perforations causes a matrix to move into position to receive molten lead and to form each letter; and the actual printing of the type on to the paper. Offset lithography is a process of photographing a pasted-up page of type, transferring the photographed image on to a plate, inking and offsetting it thence via a 'blanket' roller on to another revolving roller, and feeding the paper into contact with the roller. Offset is a versatile process, but it is only economically suitable in certain cases, since it involves an extra operation to letterpress—photographing the type, which has had to be set up as for letterpress before it can be photographed.

The most significant typographic development of recent years has been the introduction of photocomposition. The change it has brought to the printing scene (and those still to come) is probably greater than any since the advent of mechanical composition. Briefly, the various systems of photocomposition offer a letter or character image to some form of camera, instead of a mould for casting metal type. The image, selected and positioned by keyboard control, is photographed and the composed matter presented on film. After correction and make-up the film is then, most commonly, printed down on to offset plates for machining.

A major advantage of photocomposition lies in the fact that from one matrix characters can be reproduced in several sizes—unlike hot metal composition, which requires a change of matrix for each type size. To this flexibility is added the further convenience of easier make-up of the composed matter, especially so when incorporated with illustrations and display matter, for the make-up is done, in effect, with scissors and paste instead of metal type. Against the several advantages (standing type is eliminated and the capital outlay on film as opposed to typemetal is infinitely less), it would seem at present that for the average book photocomposition is inclined to be expensive when compared with hot-metal setting—but time may change this.

Offset is used mainly for long runs, where the cheaper machining process counteracts the extra cost of photography, or for short-run

reprints of copy already in type. The other common application for
offset is in heavily illustrated books, especially those with colour illustrations, whereby all block costs are avoided. The type has to be set
up and a 'repro pull' sent to the publisher, who then puts each page
of the book together, photographs included, with scissors and paste,
ready for photography. In some international editions of art books
published simultaneously by publishers in different countries the
illustrations for all the editions are printed together by colour lithography and the textual commentary set up by each publisher in his
own language and printed letterpress.

Having selected the process he proposes to use in the printing, the
production manager must draw up a composition specification for the
printer. He prepares the preliminary pages—half-title, title page,
imprint page, contents page, illustrations list, preface, etc.—perhaps
calling on a professional typographer if the book merits outside design
work, but more probably specifying the type sizes and preparing the
layouts himself. He selects a typeface and size for the text, bearing in
mind both the character of the book and the ranges of typefaces held
by the printer. The whole manuscript has to be carefully scanned and
typographical instructions given for such things as chapter headings,
running titles, book titles mentioned in the text, indented matter,
footnotes, references, tables and any other non-textual material, so
that the compositor is in no doubt about what is required as he works
his way through the manuscript. With straightforward books which
do not have sub-headings in the text, footnotes or, say, mathematical
formulae, a general instruction to the printer may be sufficient.

A printer chosen is then invited to estimate the cost of the job,
based on the detailed specification and sight of the manuscript. He
will be held to his estimate when the job is done and the account
rendered. Jobs are seldom put out to general tender among several
printers, both because of the difficulties of accurate estimating without a sight of copy and because a range of quotations is not necessary.
The production manager must know the general prices of each of his
printers and the price area in which he wishes to buy for each job. A
detailed estimate is needed for accurate costing rather than to determine whether a printer shall be offered the job. Usually the printer
is also requested to 'cast off' the manuscript—to work out the number

of pages which it will make in the type size and face specified. Accurate casting off is essential if the estimate of production costs is to prove correct when the work is completed, and most printers have a formula for each typeface which enables them to calculate fairly closely the nearest 'even working'. An even working implies a complete signature of sixteen or thirty-two pages. The smallest signature that can be sewn by the binder is a four-page signature, although a single leaf (two pages) can, of course, be 'tipped in'—glued into position. The method of 'working' is important, because the more pages that can be fitted into each forme, the fewer the number of print runs for the machine and the cheaper the printing. Thus, to print a book of 224 pages in seven formes of 32 pages is cheaper than in fourteen formes of 16 pages—double the machine time. Printers' charges are based on 'machine time'. Each item of equipment in the print shop has an hourly cost rate calculated for it, including the wages of its operatives and a proportion of general overheads. This is the hourly sum which each machine has to earn to keep the firm profitable, and it is from this that a printer estimates the cost of each job.

The specification from the production manager gives the format and size of the book, the size and type of paper to be used in the printing (see below, pp. 122–123), the typefaces to be used for display, text, footnotes, quotations, captions and index, as well as the actual type area on the page, the number of sets of proofs required, galley and page, the number and type of illustrations or the space to be allowed for them, how many preliminary pages must be allowed for, any general setting instructions to be taken into account and finally the number of copies to be printed. The specification will probably ask for the estimate to be broken down into composition, machining and binding.

The binding specification states the number of sections, the weight of case boards, the material to be used to cover them, whether the sections of the book are to be sewn and how many pages there are in each section, the style for blocking the title on the outside of the book and whether the book is to be jacketed. Such embellishments as staining the tops of the pages with a coloured ink, headbanding, or binding in a bookmark or tape will also be specified.

The most common formats in octavo size books are demy (giving a trimmed page size of $8\frac{1}{2}$ in. by $5\frac{1}{2}$ in.) and crown (giving a trimmed size of $7\frac{1}{4}$ in. by $4\frac{7}{8}$ in.). The binding case protrudes a further $\frac{1}{8}$ in. beyond the page on the three open sides. Paper sizes and the folded sizes of books which can be produced from them are shown in Fig. 13.

FIG. 13. PAPER SIZES
(in inches, depth × width)

(A) BRITISH

	Quad	Double	Trimmed Quarto	Trimmed Octavo
Royal	20×25	40×50	25×40	$12\frac{1}{4} \times 9\frac{7}{8}$	$9\frac{3}{4} \times 6\frac{1}{8}$
Medium	18×23	36×46	23×36	$11\frac{1}{4} \times 8\frac{7}{8}$	$8\frac{3}{4} \times 5\frac{5}{8}$
Demy	$17\frac{1}{2} \times 22\frac{1}{2}$	35×45	$22\frac{1}{2} \times 35$	$11 \times 8\frac{5}{8}$	$8\frac{1}{2} \times 5\frac{1}{4}$
Large Post	$16\frac{1}{2} \times 21$	33×42	21×33	$10\frac{1}{4} \times 8\frac{1}{8}$	$8 \times 5\frac{1}{8}$
Crown	15×20	30×40	20×30	$9\frac{3}{4} \times 7\frac{7}{8}$	$7\frac{1}{4} \times 4\frac{7}{8}$
Foolscap	$13\frac{1}{2} \times 17$	27×34	17×27	$8\frac{1}{4} \times 6\frac{5}{8}$	$6\frac{1}{2} \times 4\frac{1}{8}$

(B) INTERNATIONAL (trimmed sizes)

A0 $33\frac{1}{8} \times 46\frac{3}{4}$ A4 $8\frac{1}{4} \times 11\frac{3}{4}$
A1 $23\frac{3}{8} \times 33\frac{1}{8}$ A5 $5\frac{7}{8} \times 8\frac{1}{4}$
A2 $16\frac{1}{2} \times 23\frac{3}{8}$ A6 $4\frac{1}{8} \times 5\frac{7}{8}$
A3 $11\frac{3}{4} \times 16\frac{1}{2}$

There are many different makes of paper for printing, but in simple terms we may say that there are three main varieties—art or coated paper, antique laid paper and offset cartridge paper.

Art and coated papers are used in connection with illustration (photographic) and colour work. The shiny coating which is mechanically applied to the basic paper receives illustrations or solid block of colour and dot tints more evenly than cartridge papers, which tend to absorb and spread the ink. Plain text type is seldom printed on art paper unless it is integral with illustrations, because art paper is more expensive than uncoated papers and print is harder to read on a shiny surface.

Eighty-five per cent of the paper used in books in Britain is antique wove or offset cartridge. The latter is usually smoother in finish, with a thin coating of surface size in order to take the flat impression from the offset cylinder and, in general, slightly more expensive than antique.

Paper is bought by weight, and there are hundreds of different papers offering variations of price, finish and surface, weight, bulk and so on. Of any one type there are seldom less than a dozen competing brands from different manufacturers, and a publisher tends to choose the paper and the supplier he knows, unless a stranger seems to offer much better quality or price.

The production manager, having chosen to print a book letterpress, has then the secondary choice between two basic methods of setting up the type—Monotype and Linotype (a third method, Intertype, is sufficiently akin to Linotype not to warrant separate discussion).

The basic difference between Monotype and Linotype setting is that the former method casts each individual letter, punctuation mark or space on a separate piece of metal, so that a spelling mistake, for example, can be corrected simply by picking out the incorrect letter from the galley and replacing it by the correct one. With Linotype, as the name suggests, the whole line is cast as one single piece of metal, a 'slug', and any alteration necessitates the resetting of the whole line.

Linotype is cast on a different machine from Monotype and is a cheaper method of setting and one which requires less time to 'make-up' into pages; but corrections to Linotype are correspondingly more expensive (unless there is more than one correction to be made to a line). Linotype is perfectly satisfactory for a straightforward piece of text without complicated setting or page references or other matter to be added at proof stage. It is often used for fiction, as well as general books, but most letterpress setting in this country is by Monotype.

Apart from more technical differences between the two methods involving sizes of letter and type body, Monotype has a different range of type faces from Linotype. In faces such as 'Baskerville' where Linotype and Monotype versions have been cut, the particular limitations of the casting machine have meant that Linotype sizes and character widths do not exactly correspond with Monotype Baskerville. Linotype 9 point Baskerville has a wider letter than Monotype 9 point Baskerville.

Two principal measurements are used when speaking of metal type. Both refer to measurements on the face of the type body, or 'shank', which carries the letter or 'character' and not to the printed letter itself. Type 'size' is measured in 'points' (approximately $\frac{1}{72}$ in.) north to south across the shank; the type width (the east to west dimension) may also be measured in points, but in the case of Monotype units of 'set' are commonly used—the 'set' being the width of each type (a condensed or economical typeface is said to be of narrow 'set'), and the 'unit' being an eighteenth part of that other dimension, the type 'size'.

Not only are some typefaces relatively narrower or broader than others, they vary, also, in their apparent size. This is principally due to variations between typefaces in another dimension, the 'x-height'. All those characters like the 'x' (m, a, c, o, etc.) which have no 'ascenders' (the upward stalk on the h, b or l) or 'descenders' (the tail on the j, p or y) give the x-height of the typeface. If the x-height is greater than average and the ascenders and descenders consequently less than average the typeface appears large, although of the same size overall as another face. The apparent largeness is not always an aid to legibility, however, and 'leading' (the space between lines) may have to be added.

The length of a line of type, the 'measure', is normally stated in 12 point 'ems', the 'em' being the width equal to the body size (the north–south dimension). A 12 point em of type is therefore 12 points square, an 'em' quadrat, or 'quad'. In practice, when 'em' is used, unqualified by size in points, it is assumed to be a 12 point em. In the U.S.A. the less ambiguous term 'pica' is more common, pica being the founder's name for 12 point type in the days before the point system came into use. A half 'em' is an 'en', a 12 point 'en' being 6 points wide. The type area of this page is 25 × 37 ems, the former being the length in 12 point ems, or pica, of the full line, the latter being the depth of the type area. Alternatively, the number of lines per page may be given in preference to the measurement in ems deep.

If additional space is needed between the lines of type (usually as an aid to legibility), strips of lead are inserted, known as 'leads'—hence the term 'leading'. For machine composition, however, the leading may be incorporated with the cast letter, so that a line of 10 point type, 2 points leaded, would in the case of machine composition be the 10 point typeface cast on a 12 point body. To reduce the leading of such a machine set page it would be necessary, therefore, to reset the complete page—there being no way of removing one point of lead per line. A page of unleaded type is said to be 'set solid'.

There are several hundred typefaces and variations available for Monotype setting, the source of many of the designs going back to the sixteenth century, and others as modern as Univers, a sans serif face first cut in 1963.

The uses of the different typefaces vary considerably. A large number were never designed as ordinary book text faces, and may not be available in smaller sizes. Their purpose is for display in headlines or for decoration. There are approximately twenty Monotype faces in common use for books, and each of these gives a distinctive appearance which may suit the character of one sort of book but not another. There is a list of the best known on pages 126–127. Both Monotype and Linotype offer decorative borders, accents, Greek letters, mathematical and other symbols which are from time to time needed in books and magazines.

The production manager selects the face which he wants for the book and the sizes in which it is to be used for text, footnotes, quotations, captions, display matter such as chapter titles (if the same face is to be used for these) and the index, if there is one. He must also specify the overall type area for each page.

The printer may supply two kinds of proofs, galley and page, the latter either in page-on-galley or as imposed pages, which are often bound up in book form.

Galley proofs are taken from the tray or galley of type after it leaves the casting machine. A galley proof is a long sheet of paper containing perhaps a hundred lines of type. Before being sent to the publisher, a set of galley proofs is read by the printer's own reader, and such setting errors as he finds are corrected and further proofs pulled.

Page proofs are either prepared after galleys have been submitted

FIG. 14. TYPE FACES

Bembo

This is roughly the order of popularity assessed by the Monotype Corporation from the British Book Production Exhibition 1964.

Baskerville

This is roughly the order of popularity assessed by the Monotype Corporation from the British Book Production Exhibition 1964.

Times New Roman

This is roughly the order of popularity assessed by the Monotype Corporation from the British Book Production Exhibition 1964.

Plantin

This is roughly the order of popularity assessed by the Monotype Corporation from the British Book Production Exhibition 1964.

Imprint

This is roughly the order of popularity assessed by the Monotype Corporation from the British Book Production Exhibition 1964.

Fournier

This is roughly the order of popularity assessed by the Monotype Corporation from the British Book Production Exhibition 1964.

Bell

This is roughly the order of popularity assessed by the Monotype Corporation from the British Book Production Exhibition 1964.

Garamond

This is roughly the order of popularity assessed by the Monotype Corporation from the British Book Production Exhibition 1964.

Perpetua

This is roughly the order of popularity assessed by the Monotype Corporation from the British Book Production Exhibition 1964.

Caslon

This is roughly the order of popularity assessed by the Monotype Corporation from the British Book Production Exhibition 1964.

Ehrhardt	This is roughly the order of popularity assessed by the Monotype Corporation from the British Book Production Exhibition 1964.
Walbaum	This is roughly the order of popularity assessed by the Monotype Corporation from the British Book Production Exhibition 1964.
Poliphilus	This is roughly the order of popularity assessed by the Monotype Corporation from the British Book Production Exhibition 1964.
Centaur	This is roughly the order of popularity assessed by the Monotype Corporation from the British Book Production Exhibition 1964.
Bodoni	**This is roughly the order of popularity assessed by the Monotype Corporation from the British Book Production Exhibition 1964.**
Gill	This is roughly the order of popularity assessed by the Monotype Corporation from the British Book Production Exhibition 1964.
Grotesque	**This is roughly the order of popularity assessed by the Monotype Corporation from the British Book Production Exhibition 1964.**

and corrected, by breaking up the galleys of type into the requisite number of lines per page, or else they may be provided straight away without prior submission of galleys to the publisher. When a book is a simple piece of text without interspersed illustrations, it is not necessary to ask for galley proofs. Indeed, many novels go straight into 'book proof'—that is to say that the first proof the publisher sees has been bound with a rough paper cover drawn on, the pages numbered, and the preliminary pages included. Page-on-galley proofs have the type broken up into pages and the proofs pulled on galley length paper, giving perhaps three or four pages on each sheet. Printers normally charge extra for each proof which a publisher asks for above six copies.

Illustrations may be of two sorts—simple line drawings, which can be printed with text, on the same paper, and photographs or illustrations carrying tones which must be etched into a metal plate or block and, in the case of letterpress, have usually to be printed on a coated paper, either art, imitation art of calendered finish.

Line blocks are commonly made by etching the lines of the drawing direct on to a piece of metal, usually zinc. The size of the original drawing may be reduced or increased by photography to fit the needs of the book designer before the block is made.

Photographs to be reproduced and printed letterpress are made into 'half-tone' blocks by a process of photographing the original through a screen, which masks the light areas and tones of the photograph and highlights the dark tones. The result when etched on to metal, usually copper and sometimes more cheaply zinc, is a number of very fine dots, larger and overlapping in the dark areas of the picture, much smaller and less closely packed in the lighter parts. A study of any printed photograph in a book or journal with the naked eye or, better still, through a magnifying glass will illustrate the principle. Different 'screens' based on the number of dots to the square inch give more or less detail. The finest screen, which can give almost perfect reproduction of detail, is 200 and requires the block to be printed with exceptional care on the highest quality coated paper if the best results are to be achieved. At the other end of the scale, most newspaper illustrations are of 65 screen. The usual screen for book illustrations is 133, sometimes 120. In addition to the half-tone screen, there are mechanical dot and line tints which may be laid over all or part of a drawing or design to give middle tones and to improve appearance. Most publishers order blocks from their own blockmakers and have them delivered to the printers.

The index cannot be prepared at the same time as the manuscript because it is a list of page references, and until the book has been made up the page numbers are not known. It is usual for the production manager to make allowance for a certain number of index pages —the author may have indicated the approximate length of the index, or it may be obvious from the type of book—in his specification so that the printer may take them into account when casting off and estimating. The type mark-up for the index will probably be specified at this stage.

The two principal ways of binding books are by sewing the sections together before 'casing in', and by cutting the backs of the sections, then holding the pages together with a flexible glue before adding the covers or cases. The first is the stronger and more lasting method and is used for most case-bound (hardcover) books. Gluing by various ingenious methods of extruding the glue and coating the backs of the sections is most often used for paperbacks, where, after the gluing together of the sections by a thermoplastic process, a paper cover is drawn on over the book, glued to the spine, and the volume trimmed 'flush' all round. The result is not intended to stand up to prolonged rough usage. The crack which is sometimes heard when a volume is opened too sharply is the glue coat fracturing; its result in sewn books is not too damaging, because the sections are still retained by the stitching, but in a paperback the ominous cracking may herald the imminent detachment of some of the pages. Research into the use of plastic adhesives has recently reduced this weakness.

The two types of casing for the collated and sewn book are cloth (or substitute) covered boards, and soft cut-flush covers which can be trimmed by the guillotine with the rest of the book. Board covers are used in two ways; first, the conventional cloth-covered book, as mentioned, with a dust jacket folded loosely round it, and second, the slightly cheaper but less widespread method of gumming the jacket instead of a cover cloth on to the board and folding its flaps over the edges. The practical result is similar in both cases, but the second is more commonly used for educational textbooks. An alternative is obtained by printing the jacket design straight on to the cover 'cloth' and dispensing with a dust jacket.

Hardcover binding involves more processes than paperback binding—the manufacture of the case from its component parts and the blocking of the book's title on to the cloth. Strawboards (occasionally millboards) are cut to size and fixed to the pre-cut piece of cloth at each side of a centre strip of card of spine width. The cloth is turned over the edges of the boards and glued down all round, and the completed case is then passed through the blocking machine to impress the title on the spine. Before any cases are made, however, one copy of the book or a paper dummy will have been folded up by the binder to show the thickness of the book and the correct spine width to be allowed on the case.

The production manager has to make several choices for his binding. The type and weight of boards to be used will determine the strength and thickness of the case as well as its cost. There are many varieties of covering material, from leather (strong, but expensive and unusual except for presentation volumes) to linen cloths (less used because of the development of cheaper materials) and the many different grades of paper-based materials and plastics.

The blocking on the case usually consists of title, author and publisher, including perhaps the publisher's device, or colophon, as it has incorrectly come to be called. A good range of coloured foils can be used for the blocking, and the lettering is stamped into the case by a brass-cutting or, if the print run is less than 1500 copies, by a zinc equivalent which is less durable than brass. Brasses are, comparatively speaking, an expensive item, and it is not therefore common to find blocking, either in foil or 'blind', extending on to the front or back of the case. Some other possible embellishments for the volume, depending on the lavishness of appearance desired, are staining the tops of the pages between the boards with coloured ink—this will sometimes seep down into the pages if very cheap quality paper is used—binding in a strip of silk as a bookmark, or the little run of chequered cord gummed across the top and bottom of the pages against the spine, called headband and footband, which, contrary to popular belief, today serves no other purpose than decoration.

The production manager must now collate all his various estimates and prices into a costing for the book, expressed both as a gross sum, and as a 'unit' cost of manufacturing each saleable copy.

On the basis of his facts and figures the final print run, the published price and the general specification for the book will be decided, and the production manager is then free to start up active production.

Unless it has already been provided with the estimates, his first task is to obtain a schedule of production from printer and binder. This will tell him when to expect the proofs he has asked for, when these must be returned to the printer with corrections, when further proofs, if needed, will be forthcoming, when paper will be required,

Fig. 15. Costing Sheet

TITLE: _____ EDITION: _____

Format: _____ Printer text: _____
Pages text: _____ illus: _____
Pages illus: _____ ends/plans etc: _____
Binding style: _____ Jacket/covers: _____
Date: _____

TEXT Fees:
Standing type:
Composition:
Blocks/stereos
Corrections:
Proofs extra:
Machining:
Press repros:
Paper:
TOTAL:

ILLUS Fees:
Blocks/plates:
Machining:
Paper:
TOTAL:

ENDS/PLANS Fees:
Blocks/plates:
Machining:
Paper:
TOTAL:

JACKET/COVER Fees:
Blocks/plates:
Colour proofs:
Machining:
Paper:
TOTAL:

BINDING Brasses:
Fold & gather:
Complete per 1000:
TOTAL:

TOTAL COSTS Text:
Illus:
Ends/plans:
Jacket:
Binding:
TOTAL:

COST PER COPY Text:
Illus:
Ends/plans:
Jacket/cover:
Binding:
TOTAL:

PUBLISHED PRICE:
ROYALTY:

131

when printing and binding will be completed. The production manager can then alert the editorial department to arrange for the author to correct his proofs in the time allowed, and can inform the publisher and sales manager so that a provisional publication date may be fixed and a sales programme planned.

With production under way the production manager's job becomes one of superintending the work which he has initiated. He watches the printing schedule and guides proofs to and from the correct recipients, including the index copy and proofs. He organises the ordering and delivery of the paper to the printer and requests an 'out-turn' sheet as a check that the paper supplied is as ordered. Until the paper has been ordered he is unlikely to give the printer a definite print number, in case any unexpected developments have arisen at the proof stage—a book-club selection, extra publicity or topicality causing the sales manager to ask for a larger printing, increased orders from abroad or larger initial book-trade orders than had been expected.

The production manager will also arrange for the manufacture of the spine brasses for the binder, having requested and approved a bound thickness dummy of the book—a check for the jacket design— and later a specimen blocked case. Shortly afterwards he issues a binding order for the quantity required in the first binding.

Very often a publisher hedges against a possible overprinting by binding up only a proportion of the edition. Further copies can be bound up quite quickly, for the binder stores the unbound sheets, and if more copies turn out to be unnecessary the saving is worthwhile. It may also be useful to have flat sheets available in case of an order for sheets from an overseas publisher or from a book club. The production manager may have to specify to his binder that the unbound copies are to be kept in flat sheets, because binders usually find it cheaper to fold and collate all the copies, even if only a proportion of them are to be cased at first. When the first bound copies have been delivered, executive control of the book passes out of the hands of the production manager. He will often be responsible for stock records and for warning publisher and sales manager if stocks are getting short. The periodic deliveries of books from binder to the publisher's warehouse are usually a production department matter; the warehouse only calls in its short-term needs, and the bulk of stock is stored by the binder at the publisher's convenience. Type (or plates if the book has been printed offset) is sometimes kept standing at the printer until there is clearly no more chance of its being used for a reprint or new edition. The printer will charge type rent (after an initial period of grace), which serves to remind the publisher that his type is occupying expensive floor space (and metal) in the print shop. The same is true of printed sheets and occasionally of bulk copies. Many textbooks which run to successive editions go on using the same type with corrections and additions for years, as long, indeed, as the type remains sufficiently unworn. Stereo moulds of the type are sometimes made, at the publisher's expense, to release the metal and to enable the pages to be perfectly recast at low cost in the future. Printers and binders also agree to make good any imperfectly printed or bound copies with which the publisher has been charged, and in the event that these cannot be perfected, an agreement between the various trade associations has provided for crediting the publisher's account with one-third of the published price of the imperfect copy.

SALES

The sales department covers both the selling and distributive operations, and also publicity and promotion. The first of these are directed at the trade customers described in Chapter 1 (pp. 8–13), while promotion is employed both to the 'trade' and to the ultimate customer for books.

The selling effort is mainly organised by travellers, or representatives, employed by the publisher full-time to cover a specific territory and show booksellers advance copies of forthcoming books, to obtain 'subscription' orders for them, or back-list orders for titles in demand, and generally to act as the main direct contact between publisher and booksellers.

Small firms occasionally employ free-lance travellers who carry a number of different lists. For that reason alone they tend to be less satisfactory than the firm's own employee.

Other sales media carried by the traveller include dustjackets, proof copies and sometimes display kits for important books.

Travellers are controlled by a sales manager, who is office-based, but will visit customers periodically as need arises. Larger firms may have more than one sales manager with his own geographical area of responsibility, and those in charge of export markets may travel overseas a good deal in the course of a year.

The sales department is intimately involved in the production of each book right from its beginning, and may often have the decisive word whether or not a book is accepted for publication. Selling begins early in the book's life—a first announcement may be made long before a commissioned book is written, for it is a primary objective of the publisher to obtain as many orders as possible in advance of publication, so as to minimise his net capital outlay on the book. It is one widely held yardstick of a book's success that, by publication date, revenue from orders received should have covered the manufacturing costs of the edition. It is another rule of thumb (no more than that!) than an unexceptional general book can be expected to sell about the same number of copies after publication as it does on subscription.

The sales department's opinion is even more decisive in any question whether to reprint a book which has sold out its first edition than in setting the quantity of copies to be printed initially.

Educational and technical publishers also employ a different kind of representative—one whose job is not to obtain orders for books, but to visit colleges and universities to discuss with lecturers the publisher's forthcoming programme, and the gaps in subject literature which lecturers would like filled. This is representation at a more sophisticated level than the bookshop traveller employs, and is longer-term, for the results of the representative's work are broad assessments of likely textbook needs over a period of time at the institutions visited, no less than 'feedback' ideas for new books which have to go through the normal editorial processes of selection and organisation.

Overseas sales are of necessity conducted on a somewhat different basis. The largest publishing firms maintain branch offices in various main export centres, from which operation is much the same as in the U.K. The majority of publishing firms, however, either appoint a 'local' representative in each territory, who handles the lists of several firms on a travelling basis, or a stockholding agent who holds copies of all the publisher's in-print titles, usually with exclusive distribution rights within his country or territory, so that orders from overseas booksellers received direct by the publisher are referred back to the local stockholder for supply. Stockholding agents receive a sufficient discount off their orders to enable them to supply their local trade at competitive terms; freelance representatives work on a commission on turnover, as is the case with their counterparts in the U.K.

Trade with the U.S.A. forms a category of its own. The size of the U.S. market permits the majority of bookselling to and from the U.K. to be done between publishers, on a basis either of reprint rights in the buying country, or the supply of bound or unbound editions printed by the originating publisher with the buying publisher's imprint on them and shipped out under an exclusive-market arrangement. The originating publisher cannot then sell his edition in the buyer's country, nor, of course, vice versa. Some 'buying-around' by booksellers in the originating country for sale to customers in the other does occur, but most booksellers respect market agreements of which they have been informed, and the practice anyway is difficult to police.

Books which do not have sufficient sales potential to warrant separate publication in the U.S.A. are traded by booksellers in the normal way. In all countries it is the practice for booksellers to 'mark-up' the original price of a book bought from overseas—nominally to cover the increased costs of handling international orders, though it may be doubted whether the practice is fully justified, at least for books which carry higher than home trade discounts. Mark-ups are usually in each country on a scale agreed between local booksellers or their associations, in order to prevent price-cutting. The validity of the British Net Book Agreement does not extend beyond the U.K., and a publisher therefore has, in theory, no control at all over the prices at which his publications are sold in other countries. Book exports have for many years hovered around 40 per cent of U.K. publishers' total sales revenue, probably representing, after allowance for higher export discounts, well over half of sales volume. In addition, many booksellers overseas order through London agents or 'confirming houses', to whom the orders are charged as U.K. turnover, although the books are destined for export. In my own firm we estimate that some 70 per cent of our sales by volume go overseas, about half of those to the U.S.A., and the market requirements (in terms of content and format) of the latter country in particular, and of other big purchasers as well, are very influential in our decisions about what to publish.

The sales department also exercises control over warehousing, sales accounting and distribution, the particular concerns being to ensure the speediest possible supply of orders, and a stern control of credit to slow-paying or defaulting customers.

It is difficult to lay down fixed rules for the organisation of the sales department beyond platitudinous statements of the obvious. Its function is the ultimate purpose of the whole business enterprise, and its influence therefore pervades all departments of the firm to a degree which is true of no other single department.

Publicity and promotion

The publisher's publicity department is usually a separate entity from the sales department, but its activities are so closely related to sales, and its sole purpose the furtherance of sales, that publicity and advertising must be regarded as part of the sales operation.

Advertising as such offers two sorts of media to the publisher—the book trade press, and the provincial and national press. Advertising is believed by few publishers to be of much positive help to sales. Trade advertising may in this respect be more successful than public advertising, but the common feeling is that the prime purpose of advertising in the trade's two principal journals is to keep a firm's image in front of the booksellers, and only incidentally to offer some support to the travellers' personal sales efforts. Advertising in the national press is undertaken as much to content authors and to impress literary agents as out of any firm belief in its sales effectiveness. The national newspapers and journals give generous attention to books in their columns, and usually offer lower advertisement rates to publishers.

By and large, publishers regard advertising expenditure as a regrettable charge on their turnover—an average allowance may be an appropriation of about 5 per cent of turnover for direct spending on all advertising and publicity material. Spread over twelve months the resulting total can provide an interesting exercise in allocation.

The main publicity device is the publisher's catalogue. This is produced, as a rule, twice yearly, one issue containing the autumn or spring season's new books, the other new books in the second half of the year, and each with a list of all the publisher's titles in print. The catalogue gives a full description of each forthcoming book, based usually on the jacket blurb, and it is mailed to booksellers and to as many private individuals as have requested it or left a readable name and address with the publisher. The catalogue is also used to a considerable extent within the trade to sell foreign and subsidiary rights to other publishers. Publishers' catalogues are interchanged, and approaches for the purchase of rights frequently made from them.

Many publishers conceive of their catalogue purely as a sales aid rather than as a reference tool which can, by simplicity of format and standardisation in such matters as size and presentation, be of active help to a bookseller faced with an enquiry from a customer.

Nevertheless it is the advance mailing of the catalogue which produces a basic subscription for each new book, at least for publishers in defined subject fields. I myself find that the half-yearly catalogue is of such importance (the number of copies sent out initially ranges between a minimum of 5000 and a maximum of 20,000—50 to 75 per cent of them overseas), that we would almost never rush through an unexpected new book for publication before it could be included in a new catalogue.

It is a pity that not all publishers attach as much importance to their catalogue mailing lists as to the catalogues. For publishers prepared to chart the idiosyncrasies of taste of each individual who writes in to inquire about a book, or for any other reason, the specialist mailing list which results can pay rich dividends. While the general returns expected from direct mail remain as constantly low as 2 per cent, it has been known for highly specialised mailing shots to attract a 20 per cent selling response, or even higher. (My own record for an extremely specialised and expensive book was forty-one identifiable sales from a mailing of ninety shots.)

The publicity department is responsible for sending out review copies of forthcoming titles to suitable newspapers and journals, and usually for dispatching the free deposit copies of each book to copyright libraries. There are six copyright libraries, one of which is entitled automatically to a copy of all books published in Britain in an edition of more than 200 copies. The others may demand free deposit.

Review copies are dispatched about four weeks before publication, to give reviewers the chance to prepare a notice by publication day. With so many thousands of titles competing for press coverage, the percentage actually reviewed is small and, in the nationals, is confined to general trade books and fiction, with a strong emphasis on the latter. Specialist titles are covered by specialist periodicals, but reviews in the latter are seldom forthcoming for many months, and it is doubtful whether more than the occasional review has a noticeable effect on sales. Finished copies of the book are sent to reviewers, and a thriving trade is done in Fleet Street in unofficial sales by recipients of unwanted review copies to bookshops and library suppliers at, on average, a third of the marked prices.

For the rest, publicity takes the form of specialist attention to each individual title. A strong feature of educational publishing is the dispatch of free or 'desk' copies to college lecturers. We make a distinction between 'desk' copies which are sent out gratis on our own initiative in mint form, and 'inspection' copies which are sent in response to a request which is unlikely to result in class use of a textbook, but may still produce a worth-while sale; inspection copies are rubber stamped as such and their return is requested when they are sent out; we usually allocate six copies for this purpose for each edition and rotate them among inspection requests. Orders resulting are placed through the customer's usual supplier.

Publicity gimmicks can sometimes be very successful. One publisher recounted a few years ago the success he achieved by spraying with scent the proofs of a biography of a well-known perfumier. Another had a fully costumed Roman centurion parading up and down Piccadilly to publicise an historical novel. Less original efforts may capitalise intelligently on the sale of subsidiary rights in the book, or a film tie-in. The possibilities suggested by each book depend on the intuition and versatility of the publicity man and his close link with the sales manager. Publicity efforts rarely stand out by themselves above the mainstream of a book's publishing progress. They are usually part of a co-operative sales effort and are methodically planned as such—with one eye firmly on the market. About the more extraordinary examples the market's views are seldom forthcoming. Booksellers on the whole tend to like gimmicks which provide a diversion from routine, but say little about the influence they have on the size of their orders.

Direct mail is a concept originally borrowed from the American book trade, in which the retailer is by-passed and the sales effort is directed straight at the customer by means of pre-planned media advertisements or previously acquired mailing list. The concept is sufficiently advanced in this country for a set of elementary rules to have become accepted and for a rather pedantic distinction to have been drawn between mail order and direct mail selling—the one involving a press advertisement with built-in order form soliciting custom, the other a mailing shot sent direct to the home of a potential customer.

The two facts that have emerged from considerable experimentation with this method of selling are first that the conventional book trade does not like direct mail, even though evidence suggests that it helps bookshop sales, especially with account customers, and secondly, that it is only suitable for books which fulfil certain basic conditions. However, most efficient booksellers maintain their own mailing list of customers who like to receive information about new books. Antiquarian and secondhand bookselling in special subject fields depends completely on customer mailing lists, which often cover customers throughout the whole world.

For publishers it is seldom worth the expense if each mailing shot directs its recipient to his nearest bookshop to make his purchase, for in such cases the publisher has to pay both mailing cost and trade discount, and the direct mail shot becomes no more than a publicity circular which works only with very specialised books and address lists. This does, however, depend on the nature of the firm's promotion policy. We, like many technical publishers, engage in no media advertising at all, but concentrate our efforts on direct mail—from single-title shots up to group shots for several books in a similar subject area, in support of the catalogue and desk copy promotion.

Orders then come back to us through the trade, but the 'double' cost is offset by lower discounts to booksellers who are not stockholders of our publications (95 per cent of our accounts).

Direct mail and mail order, particularly of non-specialist books, is subject to certain rules. The first of these is that a return of more than 2 per cent of the numbers mailed should not be anticipated; that is the average return on general mailings, and has been obtained from numerous researches. This factor gives rise to the rule that, if only two shots in every 100 postings result in a sale, the cost of obtaining each sale is the cost of sending out fifty shots, which is high: therefore only books with a high published price can be economically sold by direct mail. The minimum price for the project to be viable has been put at about £3–5, on the basis of the production cost being up to 25 per cent of the published price, including author's royalty. In practice, most users of direct mail for books seek to insure against the long odds by multiple-purchase mailing, in which the customer is offered a choice of several books, to be bought either simultaneously or at intervals over a period. This is the way book clubs and gramophone-record clubs operate.

It is obvious that this kind of exploitation can be undertaken only by publishers with enough titles suitable for direct mail selling, or by those who tailor their lists, as book clubs do, expressly to the requirements of the method. In America some books are published specifically for mail-order selling, and to cover the mailing costs their prices may have to be higher than comparable publications for book-trade distribution. There is not yet available any detailed market-research as to the types of books which succeed best; each publisher has different experience according to the nature of his list.

There can be little doubt that the more specialised the publisher's list, the more likely is he to be successful with direct mail activity, because his potential customers can more easily be identified and reached without the wastage inevitable for general book promotion in this form.

As specialist publishing develops in scale, this direct publisher–reader information link grows accordingly, so inevitably the retail bookseller becomes more a channel of distribution than a sales initiator. His precise role and just reward for such a function is a matter of hot controversy, but for the method of selling outlined it is certainly not automatically necessary for a retailer to maintain expensive shop premises and heavy capital investment in stock to keep his shelves full.

It is because of the decline in economic importance to the publishing industry of random retail bookselling, that this section has devoted more attention to book promotion (which implies a direct link with the customer) than to trade sales methods (where the selling effort stops effectively at the bookseller). But a growth of direct contact between publisher and customer does not presage the disappearance of the book*seller*.

CHAPTER 5

THE FUTURE FOR BOOKS

IN CHAPTER 1 I sought to describe the present situation of the book
and the kind of role which it and its contributors fulfil in the
communication process today. Then followed chapters devoted to
practical techniques.

Now, if those techniques and the product which they are designed
to create are to have any continuing relevance during the coming
decades, it is desirable to re-examine the situation described in
Chapter 1 and to see whether workable conclusions can be drawn
about the way the book industry may progress in the medium-term
future.

The question to be considered is the extent to which the book will
either increase, or maintain, or begin to lose its contemporary level of
significance as a medium of communication—in other words, what
role is it likely to play?

INCREASED SIGNIFICANCE?

It is hard to conclude, from the evidence which we have, that the
book is going to increase its share of the communication process.
There are two grounds for this view—past performance and the
competition of other media.

Past performance

In Chapter 1 I gave some comparative price increases between 1955
and 1967 for: books (140 per cent), average weekly wage rates (83 per

cent), gross national product (93 per cent), the retail price index (42 per cent), and some others. It is obvious from these figures that the rise in book prices was inflationary, in that it exceeded handsomely both the GNP growth and the average rise in all retail prices, and quite severely inflationary at that. The important question about this was whether the book-price rise was the consequence of demand-inflation, or of cost-push inflation—in other words, whether prices rose to meet the levels which the market was prepared to pay (a profit-expansion situation), or whether they were forced up in order to cover increased production costs, irrespective of customer-willing-ness to pay the higher prices (a market-risk situation). Two rough yardsticks for assessing which of these was the case (at least more than the other—demand-inflation and cost-inflation are not mutually ex-clusive) are the general increase in profitability of the book-publish-ing industry over the period under review (as a result of the widening of margins permitted by expanded market demand), and the growth in numbers of books sold.

The kind of profitability we are looking for is the return on capital employed, not mere increases in the sum of the profits, and the increase in volume sales, in the same way, needs to be *per title*, not the gross sales of the increased title output during the period. The two discarded standards might reveal an increase in the volume of publishing activity, as industrial activity everywhere similarly increased, but not the achievement of a greater share of the market.

Comprehensive statistics for the book-publishing industry alone are more or less impossible to obtain. Most official sources lump book publishing in with 'the paper printing and publishing industries'. This wide-ranging group showed regular increases in overall return on capital employed from 1955 to 1967, but only detailed exam-ination of the results of several hundred book-publishing firms over the period would reveal whether their contribution to the group figure was higher or lower than average. Generally observable indi-cators like the rise to prosperity of individul firms, or common trade opinion that the book industry was booming in terms of profit return, did not noticeably suggest that books were catching up ground from the other competing media.

As far as volume sales are concerned, statistics are not formally available, but there is a simple mathematical calculation which can be used to give at least a general indication of U.K. sales trends over the period 1955–65. This calculation employs the official annual total of book publishers' sales turnover, and the average price of new titles published in a year to produce a comparative figure for the total number of copies sold in a year. Since the turnover figure represents post-discount revenue, and the average title-price is for new books only, the calculation rests upon the two presumptions that, on the one hand, general levels of trade discount remained fairly constant, and on the other, the ratio of back-list turnover to new title turnover also remained fairly constant from year to year. Both these assumptions are arguably valid provided we remember that the result of the calculation is to provide an indication of sales trends, not an exact statistic.

The actual calculation, therefore, is as follows:

In 1955 publishers' U.K. trade turnover was £31·25 million. The average price of new books published in 1955 was 12s. 1½d. We ignore, for both years 1955 and 1965, the fact that publishers' turnover is derived after trade discount, and that the published price is retail (i.e. with trade discount 'added back'), and by dividing the turnover by the average price, we reach a 'national' number of books sold in 1955 of 52 million. In 1965 turnover was £58·75 million, the average price was 28s. 7d., so the comparable national volume sale was 41 million copies, a fall over ten years of 20 per cent, or 11 million copies. An increase in numbers of books apparently sold, according to this exercise, is non-existent!

Now we go one step further. In 1955, 18,000 new titles were published, and (with the same provisos as before) if we divide the 1955 total of books sold (52 million) by the number of titles published, we arrive at a national sale of 2900 copies per title. The same calculation for 1967 (25,000 new titles) produces a sale of 1650 copies per title, a decrease of 1250 copies, or 44 per cent, in twelve years!

However inexact, of necessity, the basic data, for comparative purposes the exercise does have some validity in allowing us to conclude that book sales did not make any significant encroachment upon the communications market; and this conclusion is reinforced when regarded alongside the growth in education and in real disposable income per head of population during the period reviewed.

We cannot adduce any evidence from past performance that in the last two decades books increased their significance among the population at large as a communication medium.

Competition of other media

I have already claimed that the principal competitor to books is television. Newspapers are not substitutes for books (though newspaper circulations, as a matter of interest, between 1955 and 1965 fell by around 10 per cent overall). The cinema has long ceased to compete with the book, and is today only the poor relation of TV. (Cinema attendances between 1955 and 1965 fell from 1182 million to 327 million.)

In the case of television, however, the competition is more directly computable. Between 1955 and 1965 the cost of a television licence rose by one-third, and *spending* by the public on radio and TV licences combined rose by no less than 160 per cent *per capita*, while the number of households containing a TV set grew from 4·5 million to 13·25 million.

It may be that the growth of TV affiliation and the growth in book sales are not related to each other causatively. I cannot myself accept this. The inevitable conclusion appears to be, not that confirmed book readers are turning to television-watching as a substitute for reading, but that the pervasiveness of television is capturing the *growth* market for communication, and books are not doing so.

MAINTAINED SIGNIFICANCE?

In this context, we must first establish what we mean by a 'maintained' level of significance. If it be true that television is capturing the main part of the growth market for communication among, in particular, young people, then the future role of the book must of necessity encompass a significance not counted entirely in numerical terms.

Let us therefore consider what are the likely uses to be made of the book form in coming years, and, first of all, recapitulate briefly the situation so far. I have suggested of three broad categories of books proposed in Chapter 1, that 'entertainment' books are under the heaviest fire of competition from visual media of communication, that specialist non-fiction does, to an extent which depends on its degree of specialisation, largely by-pass direct competition from visual media, and that educational books become increasingly subordinated to, but not replaced by, visual media.

Let us look a little more closely now at these three categories. It is difficult to see 'entertainment' books maintaining even their present level of popular support in the face of videographic development. The advent of EVR (already mentioned), as a commercial product available to the public at large, has the primary consequence that the television viewer is given the choice of what he watches. At the present time choice of what is shown lies with the broadcasters, even though their selections are based primarily on maximum satisfaction of viewers' known or imputed preferences. But the change in exercise of choice of programme will put EVR tapes on an identical footing with books as far as consumer-selection is concerned, probably without even a price disadvantage, and certainly supported by public library holdings of tapes. If it is true that what I have called the 'visual' forms of communication are more readily acceptable to the bulk of the population than the 'imaginative' forms, then it is impossible not to conclude that the eventual development of a range of EVR entertainment material as wide as present-day published literature will completely displace that literature, save for a declining minority of people whose intellectual persuasions or nostalgias oblige them to continue to read books.

In this context, the attitude of authors is equally significant. The market for communication will depend inevitably upon what exists for its consumption. Will the writers of books, whether their motivations be aesthetic or commercial, continue for long to produce novels which they know will sell in declining numbers to a declining audience, when it becomes apparent that the same creative processes can be more economically rewarding (and perhaps no less aesthetically satisfying) if they are directed towards the new expanding media? Writing a book is hard work, wearying, time-consuming, and ill-rewarded. Few authors write only for their own satisfaction, and most for the readership they hope to command. Look again at the remark by Julian Mitchell quoted on page 3; it is early days yet in the progress of electronic forms of communication, and the attitude which Mitchell expressed several years ago surely cannot fail to become more widespread among creative writers as time progresses.

For specialist non-fiction and for educational books, the prospects for maintaining a role in communication are less bleak, but the role depends on the extent to which they accommodate themselves to the growth of visual media, instead of pretending that they do not exist.

In a situation in which active and current communication emerges increasingly from the visual media, one position for books is, paradoxically, further consolidated—as objects, broadly, of record. This is not to say that EVR tapes, for example, are transitory objects, or that they may not contain information which can be viewed again and again. But, in the nature of special interests, books can be more convenient forms of information storage than tapes, more easily consulted quickly or conveniently. It is entirely reasonable to foresee that a subject specialist—whether his interest be nineteenth-century American postage stamps or gardening—will continue to depend on books in large measure to support his interest, however varied may be the visual aids produced for his consumption.

In education, a parallel situation can be expected to exist. Electronic materials are already increasingly used in lecture halls and classrooms. They depend, at present, on expensive hardware outside the financial resources or inclinations of the majority of students. Commercially marketed EVR players attachable to ordinary TV sets will overcome this market disadvantage very quickly, but it should nevertheless remain true that books as a support form for educational courses will subsist for years to come. They may disappear when economic development and educational theory eventually coincide to permit dependence on technological method exclusively, but it is difficult to foresee that this will be the case for several decades yet.

Whether, therefore, for these latter two categories of book form it is possible to claim that their significance will be maintained is a more relative than absolute question. In the numerical terms of copies sold, the answer may be a negative or qualified one; in terms of the dependence of subject specialists and students upon books for the pursuit of their future interests, it may be argued that books will retain a central importance for some time to come, according (as has always been the case) to the relevance of the books which are available to those interests.

DECLINING SIGNIFICANCE?

The foregoing paragraphs have, in effect, negated the validity of this question, if books are examined according to the different categories which they comprise.

If, however, one simply considers 'a book' as a communication medium—like 'a newspaper' or 'a cinematographic film'—the general answer must be that the significance of books in the overall communications process has been in steady decline for some years, and that no circumstances, short of the voluntary destruction by society throughout the world of all the means of technological advance, are likely either to halt or reverse that decline.

In terms of mass-communication—by which I mean only communication among the majority of the population, not some derogatory classification implying low or undiscriminating intellectual levels of existence—books as we know them are on the way out, however gradual may be their exit.

The question then presents itself: what are the medium- and long-term implications of this situation for book publishers?

There are two answers, both obvious, and both dependent upon the primary assumption from which this book has been written: the book is a form of communication, it is not *itself* communication.

Specialist publishing

As a general rule it is the small or new publishing firms which tend first to work a new subject vein for books; but not always so. By exploiting the increased affluence and greater leisure which, for most people, came about from the 1950s onwards, Paul Hamlyn built up an enormous list of low-priced books on a wide range of popular subjects to cater for the 'leisure market'. The operation was highly successful, and if it seems from the outside view that it has become less so in recent years, a contributory factor may well be that a 'leisure' interest seldom remains static; it is either discarded or developed, and if the latter is the case, then development of the interest demands books of increasing depth and sophistication within the subject. For example, if as a child you begin to collect postage stamps, you happily stick into your album at first more or less anything you come across; then you look for 'sets', later stamps of a particular period or country and, if the interest is retained, you may end up like one life-long philatelist, of whom I heard recently, who collects only different specimens of the same single stamp.

I have presupposed that the main line of book publishing in the future will concentrate on identifying specific or specialised interests and activities within which there is market potential or demand for information in book form. There are two factors to consider here— selection of subjects and level of participation.

SELECTION OF SUBJECTS. There are no new subjects, in terms of a market potential which is likely to be economically viable for new book publishing—there are only gaps in existing subjects and re-presentations of existing subjects.

Many of the gaps which can be found are the result of fragmentation of subjects, as a result both of new lines of independent development, and of re-presentation of old material. My own first subject field of publishing, librarianship, offers an excellent example of fragmentation in recent years, not only through the development of 'breakaway' disciplines like 'documentation' (see p. 16 above), but also within the constituent disciplines of the whole activity— classification, cataloguing, book selection, and so on, where the state of the art develops to reveal additional facets in response to changing professional or social needs. 'Knowledge breeds knowledge', with a comfortingly exponential inevitability that offers considerable scope for the merchants of communication, book publishers (thus far) first among them, for a variety of reasons.

At the same time as knowledge expands, existing knowledge is capable of reinterpretation and re-presentation, either justified on their own account by changes, say, in fashion or style (not excluding physical style—for example, how to play golf in pictures instead of in prose), or because of a particular market opportunity.

One quite substantial example of the latter has been the phenomenon in recent years of 'sponsored' books, whereby a non-publish-
ing organisation may finance wholly or partly an artificially low-
priced publication for the advertisement value which the sponsor
obtains. There are many variations of the principle, which is simply
that the publisher is hiring out his book production and marketing
skills for a quantified return, which both removes all or most of the
speculative element of new book publishing, and avoids the initial
capital investment. Sponsorship has mainly occurred of books with
subjects which command high reader-potential, for obvious reasons,
but it occurs, too, with more limited circulation works like company
histories.

LEVEL OF PARTICIPATION. This phrase represents the degree of
specialisation within a chosen subject which the publisher considers
it desirable to cater for. Between *Gardening for Beginners* and *Commercial Breeding of Hybrid Tea Roses* (if such be possible) there
remains an enormous span of horticultural activity, in which the
number of potential readers is obviously greatest at the popular end
and lowest at the specialist end, but in which also the number of
economic *purchasers* is, paradoxically, higher at the specialist end
than at the popular one. The word 'economic' is important. The publisher of *Gardening for Beginners* is obliged to assume for such a
broad subject a wide potential readership, and one, moreover, which
is probably unwilling to pay a high price for an introductory book
which will almost certainly have numerous competitors on the lists of
other publishers; if he publishes at all, therefore, it will probably be
in a sizeable edition (which would be necessary to keep the price
down also) for a very undefined market—novice gardeners—which it
will be hard to reach by sales promotion without heavy wastage (how
do you discover the identity of all the novice gardeners in the
country?).

Commercial breeders of hybrid tea roses, on the other hand, cannot be a numerous body (if, I repeat, such an activity exists), and it is
likely that they will have some kind of professional or trade association
through which their numbers and identities can be determined and to
whom notice of the book can be sent.

So the novice-gardener publisher has the bigger potential return if his speculation pays off, but the tea-rose man has reduced his speculation to the minimum, because the size of his edition can be directly matched with the size of the market potential. Indeed, he may not in the end make less profit than his successfully speculating counterpart, because his book will be much more highly priced, both because of its smaller edition and because in a highly specialised subject the demand-inflation opportunity referred to earlier allows him greater flexibility in fixing his margins.

The ideal exploitation therefore of special-interest publishing is to match the existence of a subject gap (either through subject fragmentation or re-presentation), with the highest degree of specialisation which exists within that gap, up to the point where the demand becomes too specialised to support the selling price necessitated by the length of the edition. If this can be achieved, then that flexibility should be used to the full, but wisely. Subject specialists will always pay for quality, but they will not (like anyone else) pay a price which is manifestly outrageous in relation to the value offered. Where flexibility exists for pricing, the publisher will begin at the highest level which he believes the market will pay and may adjust the actual price downwards from that according to the single criterion of what he himself wishes to obtain from the venture, in terms of profit, publicity or public relations 'image'.

Non-book publishing

The second implication of a declining role for books in the future is that publishers should diversify into the areas of *non-book* publishing which will match up with the market demand induced by technological development.

There is nothing revolutionary about this. Many, perhaps most, of the largest book-publishing firms have been producing non-book materials of one kind and another for years—filmstrips, loops, slides, charts, packaged teaching kits, and so on—and a number of them have substantial investments of several years' standing in the new media (like EVR) which are only now coming into initial trial stages. So accustomed, indeed, is the publishing industry to the constant harangues about 'non-book media', that sectors of it have become quite jaundiced on the subject, and some few fingers have been singed by premature and unresearched ventures into the field.

Until the educational trends of the 1970s and 1980s become clearer about the emphasis which will be placed upon the use of mechanical aids in the teaching process, advance investment in this area of the market will be cautious. In the market for 'popular' communication, however, it seems fairly safe to bet on EVR as an explosive medium, though of the several methods of EVR at present under development, using different hardware, no single one has yet emerged as front-runner. (It is not unlike the 425/625 line controversy which engaged the television industry some years ago, and, more recently, the colour-television system debate.)

There is really only one point to be made about non-book media as objects for commercial publication. Although investment in them has hitherto been confined to the largest organisations, or to smaller firms which have concentrated entirely upon them (invariably through collaboration in advance with potential users, such as education authorities), there is no reason why this should continue to be the case in the future.

Once the hardware (the re-player of tapes, for example) is widely available, then the production of tapes for it should become virtually identical with the way in which books are published today. There is no suggestion that manufacturing costs of tapes will only permit long-run production or high-priced products. The openings for large or small-scale 'visual' publishing should be just as numerous as they are today for books.

I said in Chapter 1 that 'The only thing which books actually "do" is encapsulate communication'. That, too, is the only thing which videotapes will do.

INDEX